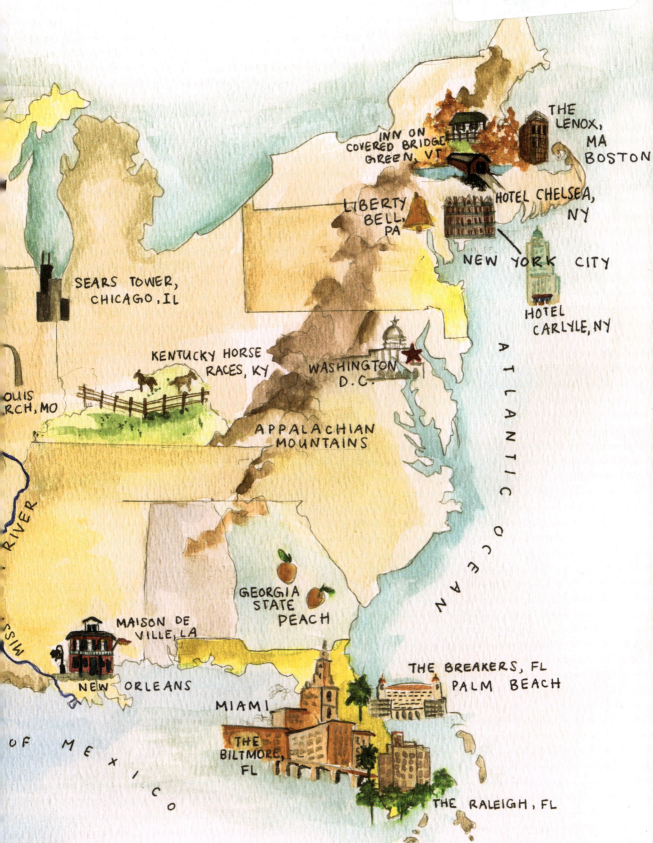

INN ON
COVERED BRIDGE
GREEN, VT

THE LENOX,
MA
BOSTON

LIBERTY
BELL,
PA

HOTEL CHELSEA,
NY

NEW YORK CITY

HOTEL
CARLYLE, NY

SEARS TOWER,
CHICAGO, IL

KENTUCKY HORSE
RACES, KY

WASHINGTON
D.C.

OUIS
RCH, MO

APPALACHIAN
MOUNTAINS

ATLANTIC OCEAN

MISS...
RIVER

GEORGIA
STATE
PEACH

MAISON DE
VILLE, LA

NEW ORLEANS

THE BREAKERS, FL
PALM BEACH

MIAMI

THE
BILTMORE,
FL

OF MEXICO

THE RALEIGH, FL

AMERICAN HOTEL STORIES

—To Bertrand

Text © Francisca Mattéoli
Translated from the French by Barbara Mellor

© 2009 Assouline Publishing
601 West 26th Street, 18th Floor
New York, NY 10001, USA
www.assouline.com

ISBN: 9 7827 5940 27 00
Cover art and endpages © April Dawn Louzek
Color Separation: Luc.A.C.Retouching
Printed in Singapore

FRANCISCA MATTÉOLI

AMERICAN HOTEL STORIES

ASSOULINE

CONTENTS

The courtyard at the Biltmore Hotel in Coral Gables, Florida.

INTRODUCTION

In 1907, my great-grandfather arrived in France from Chile and booked himself into the Hôtel du Louvre, opposite the Comédie Française. There he was to live for the rest of his life. Over half a century later, my parents and grandparents, my sister and I also checked into the same hotel, just a few rooms away from my great-grandfather's. Fate decreed that my grandfather would die at the Hôtel du Louvre, like his father before him, whereupon my grandmother checked into the Hôtel Brighton on rue de Rivoli, just a stone's throw away. There she lived for over a decade, in a little room on the fourth floor that contained a few of her belongings, a television, her precious Camel cigarettes, and any Spanish magazines she could find. I remember going to visit this old lady, by then over eighty years old, who would wait for me in the lobby, sitting there in her navy suit, always made up and with very long scarlet fingernails. After lunch in a neighboring bistro, she would go back up to her room, her decompression chamber between South America and France.

My books pay homage to these and other hotels scattered throughout the five continents, including all those that I have stayed in across the length and breadth of the United States, which have prompted this book. Few establishments manage to combine such disparate elements—drop-dead Hollywood glamour, resonant historical and literary associations, and unabashed flamboyance—with as much panache as American hotels. And few accomplish the transition from the past to the future with such stylish ease, making any author reach for superlatives.

Like the American hotels it features, this book is many things at once. Both a guidebook and a portmanteau of travelers' tales, it recounts stories from yesterday and today, leaping nimbly between genres, and including everything from practical details to the stuff of myths and legends. Just like modern journeys, in fact.

—Francisca Mattéoli

A tower suite at The Mondrian in Miami, Florida.

THE RALEIGH
Esther Williams

The fact that The Raleigh offers a suite named after Esther Williams comes as no surprise. No star could be more perfectly suited to Miami, its tropical aesthetic and its eternal sunshine, nor to the photogenic glamour of this quintessentially Art Deco hotel, whose scallop-shaped pool she made famous with her astonishing Hollywood water ballets.

Built in 1940 by the renowned architect Lawrence Murray Dixon, the Raleigh was born into the golden age of musical comedy. This was the era that saw the emergence of glamorous movie stars and jaw-dropping film sets—and it was also the age of Art Deco, when Miami hotels such as The Raleigh; The Leslie, built in 1937, The Cardozo of 1939; and The Carlyle, built in 1941, came to define the lustrous sophistication of both the style and the town.

In 1948, Williams filmed *On an Island with You* among the exotic pools of Florida's Cypress Gardens, with a scenario featuring the pyramids of water-skiers so beloved by postcard collectors today. The following year, she returned to film *Neptune's Daughter* at Weeki Wachee Springs, another paradise for mermaids. According to legend, the pool

at The Raleigh was built specially for her by MGM Studios, with whom she was under contract. And you only have to look at this astonishing palm-tree-fringed turquoise lagoon to imagine her making her spectacular appearance, surrounded by hundreds of swimmers, divers, singers, and special effects, but ultimately requiring nothing more than simply to be herself, pretty, wholesome, and sporty, with a smile that could light up the town. If travel means savoring a change of scene and a chance to have fun, enjoying a little escapism and frivolity, indulging in make-believe and casting off the shackles of everyday routine, then believe me, this is the place to fulfill all those promises.

Nearly sixty years later, The Raleigh's celebrated tropical lagoon still sees many actresses, as well as designers, stylists, artists of all descriptions, and processions of art collectors and gallery owners who come in search of dreams in a different form at Art Basel Miami Beach. This is the colorful and eclectic cast of characters that rubs shoulders on the capacious sun loungers, around the bar and in the lobby, recently restored to its original Art Deco glory. In 1944, Williams appeared—in a

A view of sparkling South Beach, located in front of The Raleigh.

Above from left: The Raleigh pool, lined with palm trees, where Esther Williams famously relaxed during visits; Williams and friends in Florida in 1955; Williams swimming in 1955. Her water performances made her a top box-office draw.

swimsuit, naturally—on the cover of *Life*, which also immortalized the lagoon as "one of the most beautiful pools in Florida."

It is exhilarating to realize that there are still hotels that pay tribute to this splendor, to the glamour of cinema's heyday, when films were the gateway to paradise, and no flight of fancy was too wild, when no amount of excess or illusion was too far-fetched, when cinema was afraid of nothing. The hotel mirrors Miami, with its impressively eclectic mix of styles, its laid-back chic, nostalgic charm, and seductive architecture.

The Raleigh's famous suite named after Esther Williams looks out over the ocean, needless to say,

and has the décor of a hotel penthouse in a 1940s film, naturally. The chorus line of sun loungers, perfectly aligned on the beach and within feet of the waves, is shaded by Deco-inspired black-and-white parasols. And not only Esther Williams but also James Bond would undoubtedly have loved the sensual intimacy of the Martini Bar. In June 2008, Karl Lagerfeld presented his resort wear collection around the pool, dedicating it to the bathing beauty whose films he had loved to watch as a child. He stayed in the Esther Williams Suite, describing the hotel as "a place that recalls the American tradition in its finest sense: old Hollywood but without the nostalgia." The finale

The Esther Williams Suite. Opposite: The facade of The Raleigh.

of his show was a breathtaking performance by the American Olympic synchronized swimming team—a reminder that this was how Esther Williams started her career. A swimming champion at the age of fifteen and holder of two world records by seventeen, she was selected to compete in the 1940 Olympics in Helsinki—which never took place because of the outbreak of war. But that's a subject for a film in and of itself...

13

ARIZONA BILTMORE

Frank Lloyd Wright

Like travel, architecture is a journey—and sometimes a legendary one. When Albert Chase McArthur, a pupil of Frank Lloyd Wright, decided to build a hotel in tribute to the master, he could never have imagined that he was creating a hotel that was totally unique. One of the Valley of the Sun's most mythical hotel complexes, the Arizona Biltmore pays wholehearted homage to Wright and leaves a powerful visual impression on visitors.

From 1907 to 1909, McArthur studied under Wright in Chicago; this experience inspired a creation that would attract every U.S. president since Herbert Hoover, as well as the elite of the business world and a galaxy of Hollywood celebrities. (Marilyn Monroe declared its pool, built in 1930, her favorite.)

Rising out of the desert like a work of art, the complex is in complete harmony with the surrounding landscape, a consummate expression of the idea of organic architecture that was so central to Wright's work and philosophy. Using natural materials that blend with the landscape, it establishes a seamless continuum between technology

The Arizona Biltmore is located in the heart of Phoenix and often called the "Jewel of the Desert."

The Aztec Room is an architectural delight with an 18-karat gold-leaf ceiling, 2 fireplaces, and a grand outdoor patio.

and an ideal of living. The scheme also illustrates Wright's passionate espousal of an architecture that was practical in all its details, as well as his uncompromising aesthetic approach. What interested him was the relationship between people and their environment; the way in which nature influences the perception and ways of thinking of those who live at the heart of it. The recurrent themes of Wright's work—the integration of buildings into the landscape, modulated ceiling heights, light flooding in through clerestories, gently sloping roofs, facades that bore the same relation to structure as flesh to bones—are all to be found at the Biltmore. And the architecture is further complemented by furnishings in a palette that evokes the desert, in shades of pink, beige, ivory, and sand. Harmonizing with all this is an oasislike garden containing sculptures by Alfonso Ianellis, which in turn stand in silent communion with the landscape.

While McArthur remained the official architect of the project, Wright monitored the plans throughout. The result is at once a modern monolith and a vast Mayan house like those that Wright would later build, constructed with concrete blocks imprinted with geometric patterns and molded on site. The outline is surrounded by forty acres of landscaped gardens. The materials used are concrete, wood, and all-natural; the rooms are immense, with a raw finish. There are two golf courses and several pools. Near to the entrance stand sculptures of sprites created by Wright in 1914 for Midway Gardens in Chicago and brought here in 1982. Following years of neglect, the Biltmore Sprites, as they have been renamed, now hold sway over the gardens like goddesses of antiquity.

Frank Lloyd Wright in 1958.

Wright working on a project with his assistants in 1958; the Adobe golf course was built in 1928 and restored in 2004; Wright's at the Biltmore is the hotel's signature historic restaurant.

> **"** *A stunning tribute to Frank Lloyd Wright, to the consummate harmony he achieved between buildings and landscape, and to his belief that 'Organic architecture seeks a superior sense of use and a finer sense of comfort, expressed in organic simplicity.'* **"**

They recall Wright's words: "Simplicity and repose are the qualities that measure the true value of any work of art."

More than six hundred guests were invited to the grand opening in 1929, when a giant wooden key (now in the Biltmore History Room) was dropped from an airplane. In the intervening years

the hotel has closed, reopened, undergone refurbishments. Twice a week, visitors can join a cultural tour of the resort. But the best way to experience it is simply to wander from room to room, pausing to admire this detail or that, breathing in the atmosphere and watching as a shaft of sunlight bisects a room like a ray of stone. After this voyage

of discovery, travelers may be moved to pay a visit to Wright's home in Scottsdale, Taliesin West, and to Gammage Auditorium on the Arizona State University Campus in Tempe, both designed by Wright, to steep themselves in all that made him one of the world's greatest architects. The journey is full of surprises, making connections between the legend and very real vision, integrated into the landscape in perfect harmony. "Organic buildings are the strength and lightness of the spiders' spinning, buildings qualified by light, bred by native character to environment, married to the ground,"

he observed. This was one of the central tenets of the school of architecture that he established in the 1930s at Taliesin West and in Wisconsin, adopting the radical educational philosophy of "learning by doing" that his aunts, Jane and Nell Lloyd-Jones, had practiced at Hillside Home School, which they founded in Wisconsin in 1886 (for which Wright designed buildings). The Arizona Biltmore stands today as an impressive testimony to his belief that "form and function should be one, joined in a spiritual union," and that ultimately, "buildings, too, are children of Earth and Sun."

HOTEL CHELSEA
Bob Dylan

Halfway along a wide street on the west side of Manhattan stands an incredible red-brick hotel. The amazing facade is half Victorian, half Gothic, with wrought-iron balconies. You can stay there for a week, a month, or a year. Many settle there for life, in rooms that are nothing like hotel rooms, which they design as works of art and create little by little in their own image, with passion. Who has stayed there? Who has lived there? Jack Kerouac, Arthur Miller, Sam Shepard, Tennessee Williams, Edith Piaf, Henri Cartier-Bresson, Leonard Cohen, Willem de Kooning, Jane Fonda, Janis Joplin, Milos Forman, Jimi Hendrix, Dennis Hopper, Robert Mapplethorpe and Patti Smith, Vladimir Nabokov, Yves Klein, Arman, Dylan Thomas—from whom Bob Dylan took his name—and who drank eighteen neat whiskeys there, his last. Arthur Clarke wrote *2001: A Space Odyssey* there. Sid Vicious stabbed his girlfriend, Nancy Spungen, in Room 100. Bob Dylan produced a record and a son there.

In 1965, when Dylan moved into Apartment 211 with his wife, Sara, whom he had secretly married, the Chelsea was the only possible choice for an artist like himself. He was already an adulated star and the hotel had already welcomed all the celebrities you could possibly think of. They were all there: Leonard Cohen, Edie Sedgewick, Warhol's Factory artists, and all the Pop Art figures. Musicians, writers, painters, and rock groups waited for the elevator, chatting, getting to know one another. Parties were regularly organized in the occupants' rooms and they were always visiting each other, going from one floor to another. Those who lived there on a monthly or yearly basis were entitled to a special rate. Some paid with sculptures or paintings, which successively decorated the foyer walls (many are still there). During the days Dylan worked on his next album. At night he went out with his musician friend Bob Neuwirth to the clubs in the Village. Sara would discover him in the morning on the divan, still fully dressed. The album *Blonde on Blonde* was released in May of 1966 and was immediately acclaimed as his masterpiece. The album was not as "angry" as previous ones, and "Sad Lady of the Lowlands," which Dylan wrote for Sara, filled up a whole side. During her stay at the Chelsea, Sara gave birth to Dylan's first son, Jesse.

The hotel's facade on 23rd Street in Manhattan's lively and legendary Chelsea neighborhood.

A view from the room where Madonna stayed upon arriving in New York in the early 1980s;
Bob Dylan in 1969; Dylan, Rick Danko, and Levon Helm, ca. 1983.

Since the 1966 release of *Chelsea Girls,* Andy Warhol's movie, the hotel has become a mythical place, exciting the imagination, giving rise to emotions hitherto unknown and continuing to attract artists from all over the world. As soon as you enter the foyer you will discover a fabulous collection of antiques, period furniture, and paintings signed by famous artists hanging on the walls around the fantastic Victorian chimney. An astonishing wrought-iron banister leads up to an antique glass dome and, as you go past the doors, you may sometimes be surprised to see children's drawings pinned up next to colored balloons, all ready for a birthday party. The apartments are still sanctuaries where people move in for quite a while. They are all furnished differently, with objects and furniture that are always unusual, complete with kitchens or kitchenettes. Don't expect to find a vast collection of bath oils, a full minibar or a Bible in the drawer of the bedside table. Everything is unexpected here, and nothing is something you may have seen elsewhere. A café, the Serena, has just been added to the old restaurant, contrasting with the rest with its modernity. Stanley Bard, the hotel director for forty-four years, has his office on the ground floor. When he is not behind the old desk with his colleagues and friends, he greets you in his dusty cubbyhole, unchanged since the 1960s, filled with bottles of drinking water, files, works by guests who have since become famous, and Bard's family photos. He doesn't give anything away easily and keeps the mystery intact. His son David and his pretty daughter Michele both work with him, just as he used to work before with his father.

Hotel Chelsea is no longer the lair of lunacy it used to be but the atmosphere remains unique: disconcerting, singularly secluded, and intimate, just like a family house—perhaps for the Addams

*The New York of Janis Joplin,
Jimi Hendrix, Robert Mapplethorpe, and Jasper Johns. A
creative cauldron, more than a hotel, where guests often
stay for a year, a few blocks from innumerable art galleries
and the Meatpacking District.*

Family, who would be delighted to welcome nephews, uncles, and cousins at any time of the year. As you go inside, a curious feeling comes over you. The feeling is of going there for an adventure, of being there to produce or create something, of an enormous sense of freedom—unexpected, nearly infinite. A few years ago the area around the hotel became the empire of trendy art galleries and French bistros that opened in the Meatpacking District warehouses. Greenwich Village is a fifteen-minute walk away and, if you follow 7th Avenue uptown, you arrive at Macy's, "the largest department store in the world," as proclaimed by the enormous sign on the store's facade. For the moment, the Hotel Chelsea has remained impervious to fashion and to change. There are strong chances it will continue to do so for quite a long time yet.

Opposite from left: Manhattan at night; looking out from the lobby of Hotel Chelsea. Below: Bob Dylan and Johnny Hallyday in 1966.

HOTEL CHELSEA

222 West 23rd Street
New York, NY 10011

TEL 1 . 212 . 243 . 3700
FAX 1 . 212 . 675 . 5531

Rooms from $300 to $390
Suites from $480 to $610

A celebrated locale for writers
and artists in a thriving
Manhattan neighborhood

www.hotelchelsea.com

RAINBOW RANCH LODGE

A River Runs Through It

As any serious devotee of fly-fishing knows, Montana is the state where you can fish some of the world's most famous rivers—Big Hole, Gallatin, Missouri, Madison, Yellowstone, Beaverhead—for kokanee salmon, perch, pike, goatfish, carp, sturgeon, moonfish, rainbow trout, lake trout, brown trout, and black-spotted cutthroat trout, the state fish of Montana. The legendary rivers of this renowned fishing area wend through the works of some of America's finest writers, including Jim Harrison, Thomas McGuane, and Richard Brautigan, all of whom have lived here or do so still.

Norman Maclean was seventy-four years old when he wrote *A River Runs Through It,* a semiautobiographical novella published in 1976, describing the lives of Norman, his younger brother, Paul, and their father, Reverend John Maclean, a Scottish Presbyterian minister and devoted fisherman, in Missoula, Montana, in the early years of the

Rainbow Ranch Lodge is located in the heart of Gallatin Canyon.

Guests on horseback in a valley carpeted with wildflowers.

twentieth century. Norman is a serious child, perhaps overly so. Paul is wild and self-destructive, entrusting everything—especially the irreparable—to chance. It is fishing, and days spent with their father among the rapids, that brings the brothers together. "In our family, there was no clear line between religion and fly-fishing," wrote Maclean. On the surface it is a tale of family and fishing. Deeper down come the symbols and metaphors so dear to Maclean: casting his line with pinpoint accuracy, Paul fishes as though he is lassoing his fish, as he might lasso life. As he fishes, Norman and his father watch. It is this delicately nuanced complicity that holds the family together.

For his film of the same name, made in 1992, director Robert Redford set some of his magnificent fishing scenes in the Livingston region, along the Gallatin River near Bozeman. Others had already suggested the idea of making a film of his novella to Maclean. The actor William Hurt, a fellow fly-fisherman, had even gone fishing with him in the hope of persuading him. In the end, Maclean told him that he was quite a good fisherman, but not good enough to play the part of his brother, as Hurt wanted to do. Maclean was won over by Redford because he promised to concentrate on the fishing. Redford narrates the tale as Norman, who is played by Craig Sheffer, while Brad Pitt plays Paul. Both actors took fishing lessons before filming, but renowned professional fly-fishermen doubled for them in the major fishing scenes. It was the young Jason Borger (who had fished from

The outdoor infinity-edge hot tub; the Pondsite Suite; the hotel offers pondside and riverside rooms, many with wood-burning river rock fireplaces.

*Famous for its restaurant
and wine cellar, horseback riding, biking, rafting,
mountain biking, and fly fishing
with professional guides in the Gallatin and
other celebrated Montana rivers.*

early childhood, was the son of a famous fisherman and had just graduated from the University of Wisconsin) who doubled for Pitt, sending his line dancing into the sky. "I grew up with fish, flies and water," he explained, and it was an image of Borger, silhouetted in the middle of the silver river as the soaring arabesques of the line he has just cast glint in the sun above him, that was chosen for the poster for the film. "It was an incredible experience," he said. "Robert Redford is himself an excellent fisherman, and he wanted to be sure everything was right." Paul's distinctive action, as described in the novella, is known as shadow casting. "Every good fisherman has a few tricks that work for him and

almost nobody else," wrote Maclean. Borger made Paul's gesture come to life in the waters of the Gallatin River, a performance which has been seen by audiences around the world and lingers indelibly in their memories.

This is the magical moment of which visitors to the Rainbow Ranch Lodge, on the Gallatin River, come in quest. Here it is, Paul's river, dancing and capering on its way from Yellowstone Park to the great Missouri River. The original ranch dates from 1919, with additions over the years that have only increased its charm. People come here not only for the fishing, the soothing atmosphere, and the sense of freedom, but also for horseback riding, climbing, and skiing. Here they can enjoy the feeling of being away from it all, the warm and welcoming country-style décor, the soft leather sofas by the fireside, the restaurant with its outstanding wine list, the view over the river, and the magnificent prairies close by with their carpets of wildflowers in spring. Elegant, easy, and unpretentious, the lodge offers a wealth of delights beside the rippling waters of the Gallatin.

THE BREAKERS PALM BEACH

Henry James

While rereading Henry James recently, I was reminded of the indispensable role that hotels play in travel writing. An account of the hotels that punctuate the books of the great travel writers—books that make you want to pack a bag, book a room, and write—would fill a volume of its own.

In 1904, Henry James was sixty years old and had not seen his native New York for two decades. He had lived in London since 1878, established his reputation as a writer, and traveled throughout Europe, or almost. But now he was overwhelmed with feelings of nostalgia and homesickness, and he decided to undertake a tour of the Unites States, visiting New York, Newport, Boston, Concord, Salem, Baltimore, Washington, Richmond, Charleston, and Florida. In 1907, he published his account of this journey, entitled *The American Scene*, studded with memories, observations, and anecdotes featuring colorful characters paired with meditations on the New World and the Old and with the feelings and emotions stirred in him by the land of his birth. And he also wrote about the hotels where he stayed, such as The Breakers at Palm Beach in Florida, established in 1896 by

Henry Morrison Flagler, the man who transformed South Florida into a major vacation destination. Describing the hotel as "vast and cool and fair, friendly, breezy, shiny, swabbed, and burnished like a royal yacht, really immaculate and delightful," James observed that "one could plunge, by a short walk through a luxuriance of garden, into the deeper depths; one could lose oneself . . . "

The hotel was first built as an annex to Flagler's original establishment, the Royal Poinciana. In 1901, after some impressive construction work, the hotel was renamed The Breakers, and soon it attracted a most distinguished clientele. In June of 1903, however, fire destroyed part of the building. Undeterred, two weeks later Flagler pledged to rebuild the hotel and reopen the following year. True to his word, in February of 1904, he opened the hotel's doors once more, this time offering four hundred and twenty-five rooms in a brand-new wooden building, with tariffs starting at four dollars a day for full board. The distinguished guest list included not only Henry James but also such names as Rockefeller, Astor, Carnegie, and Morgan: a clientele as glittering as the décor.

The grand lobby of The Breakers features a ceiling painted in 1926 reminiscent of a Renaissance villa.

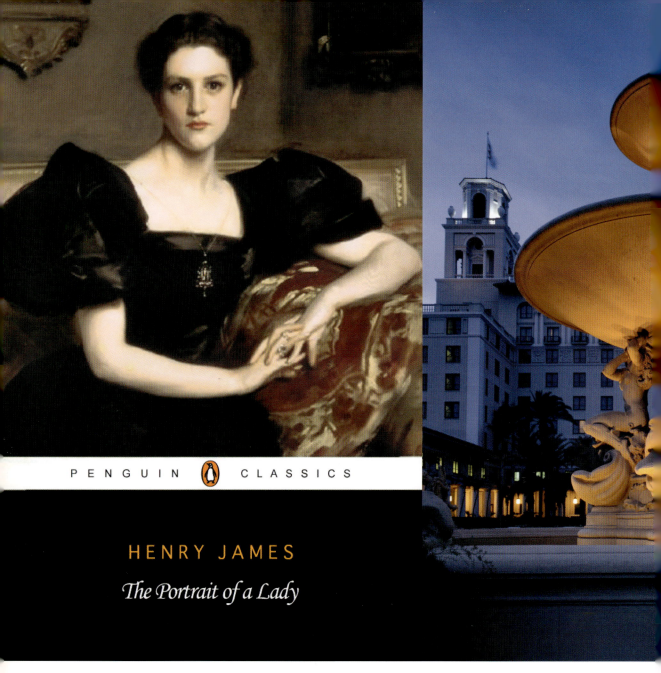

PENGUIN CLASSICS

HENRY JAMES

The Portrait of a Lady

The jacket cover of James's *Portrait of a Lady,* first published in 1881; the fountain located on the main drive of the hotel; Henry James, ca. early 1900s.

Throughout its many vicissitudes, the hotel has lost nothing of its special aura. Today's Renaissance-style building, constructed after another fire in 1925, is just as imposing and surreal as the original. Dream-like and sumptuous, it features precious furniture in the recently refurbished bedrooms and monumental lounges inspired by the Palazzo Davanzati in Florence, which have earned it a place on the National Register of Historic Places. Dazzled guests are then faced with the choice of how to spend their day: in their vast bedrooms overlooking the ocean; on the Flagler Club terrace, beside one of the pools fringed by tropical plants; in a bungalow opening onto the beach; or in the legendary lobby, inspired

Opened in 1896, The Breakers grew up
with Palm Beach. Its dazzling décor, inspired by the
finest Florentine Renaissance palazzi,
has seduced a glittering clientele, including the Vanderbilts,
Astors, Morgans, and Rockefellers.

The hotel's outdoor deck. Opposite: A bird's-eye view of The Breakers.

by the great hall of the Palazzo Carega in Genoa. The resort also features an eighteen-hole golf course, the Breakers Junior Gold Academy, a spa, luxury shops, and staff fluent in virtually every language in the world.

Whatever the many luxuries and facilities that attract today's visitors, The Breakers came into being along with Palm Beach, and therein lies its strength. The two grew up together, in the same spirit of eccentricity, with the same fierce determination to capture the hearts of travelers. And all thanks to the vision and perseverance of Henry Flagler, who decided to transform this region of what was then farmland, to bring the railroad to attract tourists, and to open this extraordinary hotel: "shiny, swabbed and burnished like a royal yacht," in the words of Henry James. Precisely so.

COLORADO TRAILS RANCH

John Wayne

Great legends never grow old. In 1861, the Pony Express carried mail for the first time on the ten-day journey from St. Louis to Sacramento. Buffalo Bill, Davy Crockett, Daniel Boone, and Kit Carson were about to enter the annals of American history. The pioneers, who were to write one of the most fascinating chapters in that history, would cross the prairies of Colorado with their wagon trains, as would the cowboys who herded cattle to new pasture on the plains, sometimes spending months in the saddle, plagued by the dust, heat, and flies. This was dangerous, poorly paid work. Rising at daybreak, the cowboys would ride in the middle of the herd, constantly fearing attacks by outlaws or Native Americans, and at the mercy of drought, storms, and floods. The rest of the year would be spent on the ranch, branding, tending, and herding the cattle, mending fences, crossing and recrossing the

An aerial view of the Colorado Trails Ranch.

Durango is a historic town surrounded by the San Juan Mountains; a man on horseback looking out at the horizon near the Colorado Trails Ranch.

> " *Live like a cowboy, join in a cattle drive, and eat around a campfire in an atmosphere worthy of a John Wayne movie.* "

same endless prairies, staying in the saddle from morning till night.

It was these cowboys who built the legend of the Wild West. And it was John Wayne, the actor from Iowa, who brought this legend to the rest of the world in the films of John Ford, Howard Hawks, Raoul Walsh, Henry Hathaway, Michael Curtis, and many others. But the true hero of these films was really the landscape. It was the main character's journey that mattered, the world that he saw, and the way of life depicted in the frontier towns that sprang up in the new territories and on the ranches covering thousands of acres. A whole culture grew up around these films, which told more than any history book could about the geography of the West and the lives of its inhabitants.

For decades, John Wayne was the cowboy, portraying the life of the early pioneers at an effortless gallop. In 1956, he made *The Searchers* with John Ford, the legendary film that started an equally legendary collaboration between the two men. *The Searchers* introduced its audiences not only

to Monument Valley, but also to the splendors of Colorado, to its mountains and valleys, to Gunnison (an early nineteenth-century cowboy settlement transformed into a military base for the film) and to Aspen, to trading posts and the Native American tribes of the plains, including the Apache, Cheyenne, Comanche, and Kiowa. In 1962, Colorado had a starring role again in perhaps the finest of all Westerns, *How the West Was Won,* with Henry Fonda, Gregory Peck, James Stewart, and Richard Widmark. This time the focus was on Durango and the Uncompahgre National Forest. In 1969, Hathaway filmed *True Grit* in several Colorado locations: Castle Rock; Montrose; Ouray; Gunnison again; the Adams Ranch, in the shadow of the San Juan mountains; and Ridgeway, the town that was Fort Smith in the film. And in 1972 came *The Cowboys,* filmed near Pagosa Springs on the banks of the San Juan River: the story of a rancher deserted by his cowboys, who takes on a group of inexperienced replacements to help him

drive a herd across the prairie, with the familiar ingredients—the immensities of the prairies and ranches, the ever-present dust—that made up the image of the Wild West.

For almost a century, the Dude Ranchers' Association has brought together ranches that set out to preserve this typically American atmosphere. The ambience at the Colorado Trails Ranch, in Durango, in the magnificent San Juan Mountains, is warm and friendly, with a simple, close-to-nature way of life and outdoor barbecues fostering camaraderie after a long day in the saddle. Guests stay in simple cabins enjoying dazzling views over the valley, and are invited to take part in cattle drives, evenings around campfires with country singers, horseback riding through the forest, watching rodeos, shoeing horses, and trying Western dancing in the Opera House. They can also take advantage of other activities, including trout fishing, archery, trap shooting, rafting, and picnics in the spectacular Mesa Verde National Park nearby.

Clockwise from left: John Wayne on the set of *Hondo,* ca. 1953; horseback riding at the Colorado Trails Ranch is one of the many activities available to guests; the Colorado Trails Ranch's own on-premises Western town.

Horse stables on the grounds of Colorado Trails Ranch.

BELLAGIO
Ocean's Eleven

It was the era of the Rat Pack, of Frank Sinatra and Dean Martin, of hotels that mixed cash with flash to create a legend. Five of the partners in crime in Lewis Milestone's 1960 film *Ocean's Eleven*—Sammy Davis Jr., Joey Bishop, and Peter Lawford, along with Martin and Sinatra—took both the hotel casinos and their cabaret stages by storm. With their velvet tones and cool swagger, they knew just how to be in the right place at the right time. The hotels in question included The Flamingo and The Sands, Shirley MacLaine made a cameo appearance, and the Rat Pack bestrode Nevada like cowboys in a Western.

Ocean's Eleven sums up an era when the Rat Pack seemed untouchable, pulling off any heist—no matter how audacious—with impunity. Except, of course, that they didn't: the cinematic criminal dream team's ambitious robbery of five different casinos on a single night was scuppered by an unforeseen twist of fate. Some forty years later, in 2001, Steven Soderbergh was to shoot a famous remake, this time setting the heist at the Bellagio.

The Bellagio stands on the site of the legendary Dunes Hotel. One of the first hotels to open in Las Vegas, in 1955, The Dunes quickly became—with The Desert Inn, The Silver Slipper, The Sahara, The Sands, and The Royal Nevada—a mythical hotel of Las Vegas's golden age. It owed its celebrity to its topless floor shows (the first in a hotel casino), its close relations with the mob, and to Frank Sinatra, who made a memorable appearance one day as a sultan riding a camel, inspired by the *Thousand and One Nights*. The publicity worked: Hollywood stars flocked to Las Vegas, and the hotel signed Cab Calloway, Maurice Chevalier, and Sophie Tucker, as well as Sinatra. This was the atmosphere and the style that the Bellagio inherited.

Clearly it was the perfect setting for the new *Ocean's Eleven*, and later for *Ocean's Thirteen*. A five-week shoot, inside and outside the hotel, would provide tremendous publicity, just like in the old days. With new sets to echo the old story, built in Los Angeles and transported to Las Vegas, where dozens of the Bellagio's technical staff, carpenters, and electricians worked to install them, the saga of Danny Ocean could be continued. The astonishing scale of the reconstruction and transformation was on a par with the legendary

The fountain's dancing waters come to life in front of the Bellagio.

George Clooney and Bernie Mac on the set of *Ocean's Eleven* in 2001.

nature of the site and its history. In one scene, moreover, as Danny Ocean stands in front of the famous Bellagio fountains with his friend Rusty Ryan, he pays homage to the Dunes Hotel and above all to its spirit.

Inspired by the Italian resort of the same name, the Bellagio is now one of the most sumptuous of Las Vegas's casino hotels. Along with the other luxury hotels of "Sin City," it embodies the spirit of this crazy town, created from nothing in the midst of one of the world's most arid deserts. Where the Sands initially had just two hundred rooms, the Bellagio offers nearly four thousand, including some five hundred suites, and employs a workforce of eight thousand. Every fifteen minutes, the fountains outside the main entrance provide a

spectacular choreographed display of water, light, and music on a massive scale, as may be seen in *Ocean's Eleven*. More entertainment of a spectacular nature is provided by Cirque de Soleil, which astonishes audiences twice daily with exclusive performances by its acrobats, swimmers, divers, and trapeze artists, reinventing the circus arts in an exhilarating combination of theater and a mystical journey. Add to all this a botanical garden nurturing more than seven thousand plants and flowers; a range of restaurants, from the ultrasophisticated to the totally relaxed; a spa with a Hollywood-style pool; and an art gallery that showcases work by renowned artists and sculptors.

The Bellagio is a pure folly that has grown like the extraordinary city it springs from, once

The Caramel Bar and Lounge.

Clockwise from above: The Cypress Suite; the cast of *Ocean's Thirteen*, 2007; a night view of the Bellagio's Mediterranean-inspired pool.

a handful of ranches and now the gambling capital of the world, a surreal extravaganza whose legendary story blends seamlessly with the wild excesses of the Rat Pack. And there's one last detail: the hotel casino, modeled on the architecture and atmosphere of an Italian palazzo and believed to be the biggest in the world. If you hear of a foolproof plan for a heist, call me.

BELLAGIO

3600 Las Vegas Blvd. South
Las Vegas, NV 89109

TEL 1 . 888 . 987 . 6667
FAX 1 . 702 . 693 . 8546

Suites from
$450 to $1,450
Penthouse from
$750 to $1,775

Dancing fountains
Conservatory & botanical gardens
Serene pools & courtyards
Bellagio Gallery of Fine Art

www.bellagio.com

SUN VALLEY LODGE

Ernest Hemingway

I remember how stunned I was on first discovering Idaho. I can still see those spectacular valleys around Boise and Ketchum, the huge summer sun over the Salmon River (known as the "river of no return" because of its fast currents), and the Wood River Valley, famous among fly-fishermen. The slopes of the great mountains were carpeted with an infinite variety of plants and flowers, and the air was filled with the scents of the land, the prairies, the forests and nearby Canada. It wasn't hard to see why so many people had decided to settle there.

This was where Ernest Hemingway spent the last years of his life, drawn by the natural wilderness, the relaxed way of life, the atmosphere of the small towns, and the hunting. He first came here in 1939, at the invitation of Averell Harriman, the magnate who had recently opened the Sun Valley Resort (with the Sun Valley Lodge as its main building). Harriman's publicist, Steve Hannagan, had

The Sun Valley Lodge pond.

Lodge in Sun Valley, Idaho; Hemingway in 1947; Bald Mountain, located just 1 1/2 miles from the Sun Valley Lodge.

Hemingway finished writing For Whom the Bell Tolls *here. The walls are covered with photographs that tell a thousand stories. A hotel that recalls the golden age of winter sports and pays tribute to the magnificent mountain landscape that surrounds it.*

the inspired idea of inviting a galaxy of celebrities and Hollywood stars to launch the hotel and ski station, a successful initiative that ensured the stars kept coming, thus guaranteeing the fame of both the ski station and the hotel.

Hemingway and his then wife, Martha Gellhorn, were given Suite 206, which he nicknamed the "Glamour House," and this was the room to which he frequently returned on his many subsequent visits. It was in this room that he put the

finishing touches on *For Whom the Bell Tolls,* his ode to the people of Spain, published in 1940. I imagine him bent over his typewriter, writing his daily quota of five hundred words in the quiet of the early morning, with the same magnificent view of the mountains outside the window that the visitor sees today. What was it about the place that he loved? All the things that make Idaho unique: its mountains, rivers, and landscapes; the isolation and outdoor life; hunting on Silver Creek; and his favorite haunts, such as the Alpine Club (now Whiskey Jacques), and the old Casino tavern in Ketchum. And it was easy to become attached to the region's relaxed, friendly charm. Having come to view his suite at the Sun Valley Lodge as home, Hemingway eventually bought a property in the Wood River Valley: his last home before the fatal shotgun wound in the heart of the mountains.

If you ask any regular visitor here which hotel best represents Sun Valley, they will almost certainly say the Sun Valley Lodge. Since its opening in 1936, it has lost none of its easy, elegant atmosphere, designed for lovers of both the outdoor life and hotels of character and spirit. The windows of the rooms look out over a landscape of mountains, trees, and unspoiled valleys, a magical sight in any season. In its early years the hotel received Claudette Colbert, Errol Flynn and their glittering contemporaries; today the stars still come, attracted by the glamorous patina of this golden age combined with all the luxuries you could hope for in a modern ski resort, such as a spa, swimming pool, flat-screen televisions, and shops. The walls of the hotel are hung with hundreds of black-and-white photographs of celebrities, which bring visitors back to the era of Lucille Ball, Gary Cooper, John Wayne, and the legendary ski champions who sealed the resort's reputation.

But the thing that still attracts visitors here from all over the world is the unique atmosphere. Seduced by long walks through the glorious

Suite 206, where Hemingway lived.
Opposite: Hemingway on his typewriter in Suite 206.

landscapes, the fishing, and the rafting, many photographers, sculptors, and actors have taken up permanent residence. The sculptor Carolyn Olbum finds inspiration here, she says, in wild, untamed nature, in all its elements, whether massive or minuscule in scale, while the softness of its colors in the morning light brings her a wonderful sense of tranquility. Her work evokes this world of raw, unmediated feeling that captivated Hemingway and inspired Ezra Pound, Richard McKenna, Patrick F. McManus, and so many other writers and artists. Who wouldn't fall in love with the setting, and with this venerable hotel—authentic, different, serenely unperturbed by the excitements of the world beyond it; ageless, timeless and beyond the reach of whim or fashion? Who could resist these landscapes and valleys, with their changing colors in summer, winter, and autumn, which make you feel so perfectly in harmony with nature?

HOTEL DEL CORONADO
Some Like It Hot

Billy Wilder had said, "I'll never work with Monroe again." He had not forgotten his dreadful experience during the filming of *The Seven Year Itch*. But the idea of having the greatest star in the universe for his next film was too tempting to resist. Said Wilder, "The genesis of the idea was a very low-budget German picture, *Fanfares of Love,* where two guys who need a job dress up in drag to get into a female band. But there was not one other thing that came from this picture." Wilder came up with the idea of situating the action "in the era of Prohibition, based around the St. Valentine's Day Massacre," with a fantastic chase to escape from gangsters, and the absolute necessity of dressing as women—"it's a question of life and death." The producer David O. Selznik did not think it was such a great idea: "You're not doing a comedy with murder? They're going to crucify you!"

Wilder disagreed. As he said, "We were pretty sure it would be a good comedy. What we did not know was that it would be a great comedy." Monroe wanted to do the part of Sugar Kane and play the ukulele in the all-girl band; Jack Lemmon and Tony Curtis had already agreed to play Josephine

and Daphne. The project was launched. Wilder and his colleague I. A. L. Diamond were bubbling with excitement. They met every day in Wilder's office at Paramount and reeled off ideas. "The sex scene on the boat between Marilyn and Tony Curtis was too predictable." They were obviously not going to make love on the screen and nothing really scandalous was going to happen. They were, however, going to do a real sex scene—really suggestive. "And she suggests the sex—that has to be better, to be seduced by Marilyn Monroe—what could be better? So she tries, and you know his real feelings by what happens to his leg, as it goes up."

The filmgoers were delighted. Three-quarters of the film featured the Hotel del Coronado, across the bay from San Diego, as a backdrop—in black and white because Wilder did not think that actors dressed in drag would work in color. The extravagant building, poised on the beach approximately two hours south of Los Angeles, had immediately enchanted him. It was the only place that hadn't changed in thirty years. In September 1958 the entire crew moved into the hotel for a week with their husbands, wives, and children.

The Hotel del Coronado's signature red turret played a prominent role in the film, and years later, *Some Like It Hot* fans still flock to stand where Marilyn Monroe stood.

The Hotel del Coronado in its peak season.
Opposite: Marilyn Monroe on the set of the film in 1958.

The movie made the most of the 1888 Victorian chef-d'oeuvre. The musicians arriving in front of the hotel and the succession of eighty-year-old millionaires sitting in their rocking chairs reading the *Wall Street Journal* (with the fabulous Joe E. Brown in the front row) was one marvelous moment. Jack Lemmon playing maracas in his room after a night dancing that memorable tango with Osgood Fielding III (Brown), imagining himself marrying and divorcing in order to get a settlement, was another. Palm trees, beaches unfolding outside the bedrooms, the colonial verandas,

the historic salons. The first meeting in the film between Monroe and Curtis, disguised as an oil magnate, on the magnificent beach in front of the Hotel del Coronado, is unmistakable among a thousand. The grand finale on the boat, when Lemmon announces to Brown's character, "I cannot marry you because I smoke . . . Look, I'm a man." And Brown dismissing these minor details with that famous one-liner: "Nobody's perfect!"

Arriving at the end of Orange Avenue, you will immediately recognize the unmistakable Hotel del Coronado, "The Del," as it is called here. A fabulous

One glance and you are definitely inside
Some Like It Hot *Fabulously extravagant and quite unmistakable, the hotel is a historic landmark two hours from Los Angeles on the Mexican border.*

The legendary chandeliers in the Crown Room were designed by
Wizard of Oz author L. Frank Baum; the hotel lobby has hosted the arrival of many historic visitors.
Opposite: An ocean view from one of the hotel's coastal cottages.

restoration has not changed this legendary luxury hotel, with its wood paneling, cane furniture and walls covered with dusky pink material. Rumor has it that Edward VIII met Wallis Simpson here. Around the hotel, the bays, Spanish missions, golf courses and sun-drenched beaches of San Diego stretch out for miles. In the historic Gaslamp Quarter, restaurants serve tacos and enchiladas (Mexico is only twenty minutes away). You really feel as if you are in a Mexican square in the Bazaar del Mundo, on Calhoun Street. Surfers will go to La Jolla, the chic area of superb villas, stores, and luxury restaurants along the coast, while parents will enjoy showing their children the wonders of Sea World, one of the biggest and most impressive aquariums in the world, twenty minutes from The Del. Those who prefer to linger in the atmosphere of the movie can book themselves in at the Hotel del Coronado and remember with emotion the famous scene in Lemmon and Curtis's room when Monroe is feverishly rummaging through a chest of drawers, asking, "Where's that bourbon?" The scene required fifty-nine takes. Finally Wilder stuck pieces of paper in all the drawers on which he had written "Where's that bourbon?"

DON CESAR BEACH RESORT

F. Scott Fitzgerald

It is the summer of 1932, and Scott and Zelda are on vacation in St. Petersburg, Florida. He had met her at a country-club ball in Montgomery, Alabama, wooed and won her, became engaged to her in 1919, and then went on to write, among other fine works, *The Great Gatsby.* In the 1920s, the couple had made several excursions to Paris and the French Riviera, living the glittering lifestyle of the decade that Fitzgerald dubbed the Jazz Age. But by the end of the decade Zelda's health was fragile, and Fitzgerald himself was suffering from alcoholism. In 1930, Zelda's schizophrenia took hold and they returned to the United States, never to leave the country again. By the time they checked into "the Don," the final act of their tragedy had already begun.

In the 1930s the "Pink Palace" was a new playground for the rich and fashionable, opened in 1928 on a gleaming white beach, a mere stone's throw from the turquoise waters of the Gulf of Florida. Chic vacationers would gather on St. Pete Beach to bathe, take

The Don CeSar is located on a stretch of shimmering white beach.

The Don is often called the "Legendary Pink Palace" for its vibrant exterior; Fitzgerald reading at his desk, ca. 1920s; guest rooms have exquisite views of the Gulf of Mexico or Boca Ciega Bay.

boat trips to the islands, and enjoy long, sybaritic picnics in the Florida sunshine. Having been introduced to the delights of sunbathing, which became fashionable in the Côte d'Azur thanks to Coco Chanel, Scott and Zelda now found the perfect time and place to indulge in this daring new pastime.

The Fitzgeralds had decided to take a few days' break from Hollywood, where Scott had been reduced to working on scripts for Metro-Goldwyn-Mayer—work that he found degrading and depressing—in order to pay off his mountainous debts. With Scott hiding his whisky bottles and Zelda becoming rapidly more unstable, subject to hallucinations and hearing voices; with each spying on the other and consumed by jealousy; with their health and finances broken by their ruinous lifestyle of extravagant excess and their future doomed, this must have been a strange holiday indeed.

The Don CeSar Beach Resort, named after Don Caesar de Bazan—the hero of the nineteenth-century British opera *Maritana,* still sits on the sparkling white beach like a pink-and-white wedding cake, just as it did on the day of its opening. There are hotels like that, that seem immune to the passing of the years, to changing fashions, to the life that goes on around them, that survive all changes and etch themselves into our memories in a way that is almost subliminal. The astonishing, unavoidable, ubiquitous pinkness of it undoubtedly has a lot to do with it. And the flamboyant architecture, the work of Henry DuPont, also lends it its own incomparable character. This is a hotel that could have been created for Jay Gatsby, and is of his time—a Jazz Age palace, complete with verandas and picture windows, tropical gardens and fountains, turrets and balconies, and breathtaking views over the Gulf of Mexico.

The hotel's guests have included Lou Gehrig, Al Capone, Clarence Darrow, Lauren Bacall, Zsa Zsa Gabor, Pink Floyd, presidents, and artists of every persuasion; but it is Scott Fitzgerald who heads the list, with all the atmosphere of outrageous excess

that infused his work. You begin to imagine some of those moments, as precious as they were short-lived, those evenings with elegant fellow guests, slightly tipsy, invariably melancholy, drowning in a surfeit of wealth and alcohol. Your thoughts turn to James Gatz/Jay Gatsby, on his palatial estate, to the flamboyant parties on the lawn, to the marble swimming pool, to pink champagne in crystal glasses, to a dreamlike setting and bizarre, sublime moments, where everything has an air of unreality.

The same is true of the Don itself, promising days "from ice cream to caviar." Turned into a hospital

66 *A witness to the grandeur and excesses of recent American history, the Pink Palace has seen everything, experienced everything—and remains as majestic, breathtaking, and surreal as it ever was.* 99

The redesigned pool deck is lined with Brazilian Ippa wood and set amid lush oleander and date palm trees.
Opposite: F. Scott Fitzgerald with his wife, Zelda, ca. late 1920s.

for airmen by the U.S. Army, from 1942 to 1945, then abandoned, it has been daubed with graffiti, forgotten—and finally, as if by a miracle, restored to life. Renovated, refurbished and brought back into operation, the Don was featured in the pages of *National Geographic,* was used as a set for Sergio Leone's film *Once Upon a Time in America,* and appeared in a Tom Petty video. A witness to the grandeur and excesses of recent American history, the Pink Palace has seen everything, experienced everything—and remains as majestic, breathtaking, and surreal as it ever was.

THE CARLYLE
Woody Allen

The Carlyle, its restaurant, and its legendary café are made for lovers with a taste for the eccentric and sophisticates with a penchant for the raffish. It is a place for those who love backdrops of Hollywood glamour, unexpected decors ranging from a Moroccan hall to a black-and-white marble lobby, and an ambience that might recall an encounter, a liaison, an anticipation, a reunion, a wise decision, or a moment of madness . . .

Dating from 1930, the Carlyle was one of the first residential hotels to open in the city. With the Algonquin, the Essex House, the Wolcott, the Pennsylvania, the Sherry-Netherland, and a handful of others, it is one of the aristocratic veterans of New York hotels. Built at a time when men of influence needed a pied-à-terre in town, it has been refurbished and modernized as a fabulously chic boutique hotel, with Empire-style rooms adorned with works by Piranesi and Audubon.

Clients of the Café Carlyle, it's said, have seen everything in life. One day, places like this—where regulars come to relive memories, to travel back in time, where ambience is everything (or nearly everything), where you can escape from the real world through the discreet little door—won't exist any more. It evokes the golden age of New York cabaret, during Prohibition, when by law alcoholic drinks could only be served with food. This was how "supper clubs" grew up—small, smoke-filled, dimly lit rooms designed to hold half the number of people who squeezed into them, where clients would spend the evening sitting at crowded tables and listening to music. The singers would perch on a tiny platform with, if they were in luck, a piano to accompany them and—the height of luxury—a microphone. The music was usually jazz or songs from Broadway musicals, and the artists, often unknown, were stars in the making. These were the perfect places, in short, to impress a girl. In the 1940s and '50s, the most popular supper clubs in New York were Tony's, Café Society (where Billie Holiday first performed), Spivy's Roof, and the Blue Angel. Then there were the ones in Greenwich Village, and those of the theater district, where former Broadway stars could join the ranks of showbiz once more. In the end, supper clubs popped up everywhere, like skyscrapers.

A view of midtown Manhattan from one of the glorious Carlyle suites.

Clockwise from above: Even today, Allen plays every Monday evening at the Carlyle; the facade on the Upper East Side; the interior of Café Carlyle.

Allen with his jazz band playing at the cafe.

Since 1955, one of the most famous has always been the Café Carlyle, racking up fifty years of memories for its faithful regulars, some of whom are reputed to have handed the flame down through the generations, from parents to children and from grandparents to grandchildren.

The traditional little tables are still there, though nowadays they are more generously spaced and extremely elegant with their white linen napery. The light is still low, but now it is soft and intimate, designed to create the feeling of a world apart and to pick out the frescoes on the walls. And the supper-club menu is still there, too: simple and easy to serve, but now refreshed, improved and inspired by international cuisine, with classics such as shrimp cocktail, Caesar salad, cheesecake, and crème brûlée—a Franco-American menu to complement the music of Cole Porter and Gershwin, just like in *Manhattan*.

> " *It is a place for those who love backdrops of Hollywood glamour, unexpected decors . . . and an ambience that might recall an encounter, a liaison, an anticipation, a reunion, a wise decision, or a moment of madness . . .* "

The entrance to the Carlyle on East 76th Street.
Opposite: The lobby of the Carlyle, designed by interior designer Dorothy Draper in the 1930s.

So it comes as no surprise to see Woody Allen here. After all, the whole neighborhood consists of backdrops to his films: Park and Lexington Avenues, E.A.T., Central Park, the Frank E. Campbell Funeral Chapel on Madison—an itinerary of legends for movie buffs. On Mondays, Woody Allen comes to play at the café with the Eddy Davis New Orleans Jazz Band, who have accompanied him for nearly a quarter of a century. Every week, they say, there's a queue of at least fifty to hear him. And to see him, naturally. From 1968 to 2005, it was Bobby Short who made the Café Carlyle what it was. Born into a poor family in Illinois, Short became a legendary crooner who embodied the essence of New York glamour with his velvet voice, impeccable dinner jacket, and sophisticated act that was at once happy and melancholy. He sang on the soundtrack of Woody Allen's *Manhattan Murder Mystery*, and played himself singing a Cole Porter song at the Carlyle in *Hannah and her Sisters*.

MISSION RANCH

Clint Eastwood

Legends are born of a curious alchemy: a feeling that permeates a place, the people who have passed through it and given it its soul, the memories that we bring to it, an unusually potent atmosphere . . . an infinite number of details, both small and large, to which everyone brings their own fantasies and discoveries. I spent ten years in Carmel, often at Mission Ranch. A madcap notion, love at first sight—call it what you will. The heady scent of the eucalyptus trees; the dusty roads engulfed in greenery; the little town so beloved by photographers, poets, writers and adventurers from the 1920s to the present day, including Sinclair Lewis, Robert Louis Stevenson, Ansel Adams, Mary Austin (who founded the Forest Theater here around 1910), Jack London, James Ellroy; the bohemian chic of the 1970s: it all conspired to make the place irresistible.

Clint Eastwood featured Mission Ranch at Carmel in his 1971 film *Play Misty for*

The Carmel Mission Basilica.

Donna Mills and Clint Eastwood in a still from *Play Misty For Me*, 1971; a view of Carmel Valley and the Carmel Valley Ranch Golf Course.

66 *A hotel full of charm and history, painstakingly restored by Clint Eastwood, in the heart of the beautiful town of Carmel, on which Mary Austin, Jack London, Sinclair Lewis, and numerous other artistic spirits have left their mark…* 99

Me. At this point he was not yet the owner of Mission Ranch, but with this first film to be shot in the town and in the Monterey region, the actor entered local mythology. Watching the film again, I rediscovered all that goes into the charm of this place and this unexpected hotel, nestled among dirt roads and sheep pastures. This is not one of those historic hotels that you can see from miles away, no sumptuous, monumental palace. It doesn't conform to the classic idea of a legendary hotel at all. And so much the better. Instead, it fits perfectly with Carmel, with its little houses in pastel colors, its beautifully tended pocket-handkerchief gardens, its wild shoreline, and its

famous forests of cypresses—twisted, bizarre, sometimes disturbing even. Built in around 1850, the ranch remained a farm until the 1920s, when it embarked on a series of incarnations as a private club, restaurant, and hotel. Gradually its fame spread, and by the 1950s its restaurant was popular locally for relaxed dinners and evenings among friends—as it still is today. Hardly have you unpacked your bags before you're tucking into the soup of the day and roast chicken. And usually someone will be there playing jazz piano, just as in *Play Misty,* accompanying the views over the surrounding landscape with tunes from Errol Garner, Roberta Flack, Johnny Otis, Gene Connors, Joe Zawinul, and the like.

Sunday jazz brunch soon became a tradition, with guests gathering around the piano to sing jazz classics. From the bedroom of one of the cottages, meanwhile, you can watch sheep cropping the pasture in a bucolic scene more reminiscent of the English countryside than California. The landscapes in the film are equally unexpected:

winter scenes, empty roads, deserted beaches fringed by cliffs. The surprises are startling. The same is true of Carmel and its surrounding region, which without its changing character—sometimes you are reminded of Scotland, sometimes of Ireland, sometimes even of South America—might be just a pretty town like any other. In the film, we visit the whole area around the ranch, from Big Sur to Carmel Valley, via Monterey, Pacific Grove, Ocean Avenue, and of course the beaches—beaches that are still unspoiled, screened by trees and rustic wooden fences, just a few minutes' walk outside the town. If you walk down Ocean Avenue, you find yourself on the sand.

In the summer, tourists come here, many of them regulars who are brave enough to bathe in the icy waters. In the evenings, guests gather beneath the heaters on the ranch patio, at one of the wooden tables or in one of the Adirondack chairs: families, neighbors from Carmel, tourists from the world over, all seeking nothing more

A bucolic scene on the ranch.
Opposite: The historic ranch dates back to the 1850s.

than to spend a happy few hours over barbecued ribs and a glass or two of Chardonnay. Some may recognize elements of the decor from their host's films. It's all friendly, simple, unpretentious. People chat between tables, happy to be there. This is the way legends are perpetuated: with countless little details, which in the end come to define the spirit of a place.

BILTMORE HOTEL
Al Capone

One of the big events of 1931 in the United States was, without a doubt, the trial and sentencing of gangster Al Capone. He showed up in court all smiles, wearing a magnificent banana-colored suit and flanked by an army of lawyers. He left with an eleven-year prison sentence and a $70,000 fine for tax evasion. He spent seven years in prison, four of them at Alcatraz.

Upon his release in 1939 for good behavior, Capone, riddled with syphilis, was told by doctors that he had only eight years to live. So the former gangster decided to treat himself to early retirement in the sunshine of Miami, already the city of high-finance tycoons, the Mafia, and stars, one of his favorite haunts before being put behind bars. At the time, he pretended to be a modest furniture salesman. He was now a quiet, retired man of forty. The Miami authorities would have preferred to manage without him, but to no avail. This was where he decided to live. He planned everything, and his routine was a very ordinary one, or so it had seemed. When he was not on his Palm Island property with his wife, Mae,

he would go fishing, showing off proudly at the stern of his yacht, bloated and jovial, a large cigar in one corner of his mouth, even serving beers to journalists who came to interview him. So as not to lose his touch, he also played cards and set up an illicit bar at the Biltmore Hotel in Coral Gables, where he always loved to stay.

This impressive building in the Spanish baroque style, only a cable's length from Miami Beach, was indeed made for him, with its monumental entrance hall, cathedral-type columns, enormous swimming pool, and overwhelming opulence. His suite in the Campanile Tower, inspired by the Giralda in Seville, Spain, is the most luxurious in the hotel. The fabulous ceiling with arcades is reminiscent of a medieval priory. The extraordinary decor, of a Moor castle; the balconies and facades, surrounded by enormous gardens, of Granada's great Alhambra. A real gangster's hideaway. Al Capone never left Miami alive. Wracked by illness, Scarface, public enemy number one, successor to the old Mafia chief Johnny Torrio, died on Palm Island on June 25, 1947, of a heart attack. His funeral was

The Biltmore's tower at night.

American gangster Al Capone relaxing in Miami in 1930.

far removed from the grandeur of his heyday. The coffin, carried by six cemetery staff, cost $2,000, and only about forty people followed the procession. Eighteen years after the St. Valentine's Day massacre and the follies of Prohibition, there was little left of the greatest criminal of all time. The Capone Suite at the Biltmore Hotel is just as it was in his day, sumptuous, stupendous, stunning, outrageous—just like Miami.

Since then Anglo-Saxons have mixed with Cubans, Jamaicans, Haitians, Nicaraguans, Salvadorans and other Latin Americans, and people in the city speak as much Spanish as they do English. The Art Deco area in South Beach has become world-renowned, with buildings designed by the greatest names in international architecture. The enchanting Coconut Grove, filled with pretty restaurants, is taken by storm every Friday by the residents of the area, who celebrate the start of the weekend with a beer or a glass of wine. The fabulous Villa Vizcaya museum, an incredible Venetian-style palace with seventy-two bedrooms surrounded by sumptuous gardens, entices, as does Coral Gables, the old Spanish area surrounding the hotel, with its French restaurants on Ponce de Leon Boulevard, its squares, fountains, and golf courses, including that of the Biltmore, right in the middle of a tropical garden.

A private poolside cabana suite nestled among palms and hibiscus.

Clockwise from top: The Everglades suite, also known as "the Al Capone Suite"; view of the hotel from 18-hole, par 71 Donald Ross golf course; the glorious loggia, which includes a fountain and palm trees; the Biltmore pool.

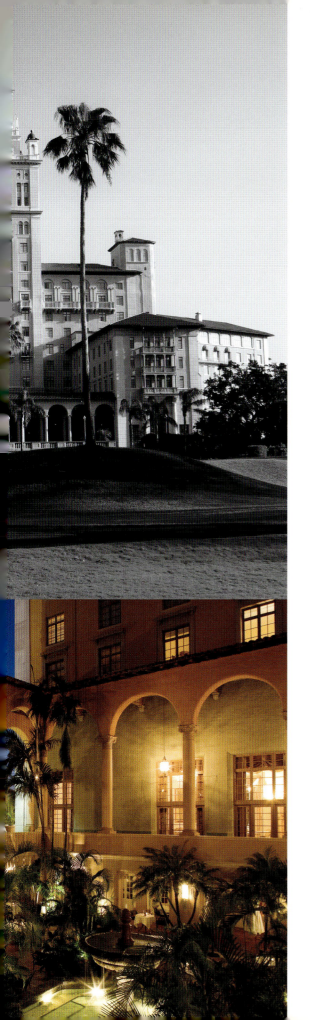

*Enormous gardens,
a tower inspired by
the Giralda in Seville,
fabulous lounges, the
country's largest hotel
swimming pool. An
amazing sight worthy of
Miami, where
extravagance reigns.*

SUNDANCE RESORT
Butch Cassidy and the Sundance Kid

A vast and protected territory lies to the west of Colorado and the Rocky Mountains. Its bare rocks, which in winter can be covered by several feet of snow, rugged mountains, tortuous canyons, and extreme temperatures have discouraged developers and individuals alike to this very day. It is wild and ideal countryside such as was discovered by the first pioneers, trappers, fur traders, and Native American tribes. Utah represents the American myth within human reach.

In 1969, Robert Redford and George Roy Hill shot a Western in these mountains, brimming over with charm and audacity, as light as a milkshake: *Butch Cassidy and the Sundance Kid,* the tale of two endearing rogues (Paul Newman and Redford) and a lovely teacher (Katharine Ross) launched on the craziest road to crime, from the Western plains to Bolivia. It was impossible to forget the superb sepia scenes, wild rivers and creeks as far as the eye could see, the atmosphere of America at the turn of the century, combined with the splendor of natural landscapes. (Newman and Redford held up a Bolivian bank with the help of a Spanish phrasebook!)

Both landscapes and atmosphere fascinated Redford to the extent that he had already purchased a little house in Utah. With his earnings from *Butch Cassidy and the Sundance Kid,* he acquired the whole valley at the foot of Mount Timpanogos, a site favored by Native Americans, who used to shelter there in very hot weather before it became the property of a family of Scottish immigrants, the Stewarts. This region was also renowned as being the stage for several major acts in the conquest of the Far West.

Redford's idea: to combine art with nature in a wild and unique context, totally protected. Over the years the project took shape, the site developed, Sundance emerged, and a hotel was born—or rather, a cluster of wooden cottages along a small road lined with gray rocks and spruces. Sundance is invisible from a distance. You need to drive some thirty-seven miles from Salt Lake City, Utah, the Mormon capital, disappear into the Middle Rockies, travel past blue lakes and alongside a small cascading river, and after approximately three miles of winding roads high up in the mountains, locate the flat stone marked "Sundance." Nothing outrageously

The exterior of Rehearsal Hall at Sundance Resort.

Clockwise from top: Alpine skiing in Utah country; Paul Newman and Katharine Ross in a still from *Butch Cassidy and the Sundance Kid*, 1969; Robert Redford and Newman on the set; Redford and Newman on horseback.

luxurious or pretentious. A simple wooden cabin full of old books and worn furniture welcomes visitors. A few copses of flowers, a small parking lot, conifer-covered mountain peaks in the distance, and even further, a vast territory deliberately left in its wild state. There is also a bar, a grocery store with produce from the Sundance farms, a snack bar, a restaurant, and other creature comforts.

Sundance disconcerts and enchants through its complete contrast with the world of Hollywood, cleverly combining the extraordinary possibilities afforded by the surrounding countryside. Even the famous Sundance Film Festival seems very far away. No need to even mention the word "environment." One glance at what has been achieved here and anywhere else on the planet seems dirty, tired, incredibly built up. Native American statues and a gigantic Navajo tapestry decorate the dining room, built around a tree, which was left intact. At the end of a small hidden pathway, two paces away from an enchanting river, appears Etta's Hideaway, a superb rustic wooden cottage, named after Katharine Ross's character in the film, where every detail is a reminder of the movie's atmosphere. Innumerable activities abound for everyone—craft workshops, a magnificent cinema, theater entertainment under the stars (for which it is best to bring one, or even two, good, thick blankets, as the temperature plummets at night—and soup is served during the intermission) superb trekking trails (described in a beautiful leaflet), a riding school on a miniature ranch, supervised by a big, jovial cowboy in leathers who knows his job and ensures that beginners are given

The resort exterior surrounded by snow-covered spruce trees.
Below: An 1896 prison profile for Butch Cassidy stating his pardon.
Opposite: A candlelit corner of the Tree Room, where memorabilia from
Robert Redford's private collection is on display.

the oldest nags. Everything takes place in a good-natured atmosphere that attracts more athletes than socialites, just a few miles away from a now legendary film festival. Art and nature have found a meeting place. An astonishing and magical place, patiently designed step by step over thirty years. With *Butch Cassidy and the Sundance Kid,* Robert Redford's dream has come true.

INN ON COVERED BRIDGE GREEN

Norman Rockwell

From 1939 to 1953, Norman Rockwell lived with his wife and three children in Arlington, Vermont. After the frantic pace of life in New York, he used to say, it was a whole different world. By this time Rockwell was already the celebrated illustrator of the *Saturday Evening Post,* renowned for his whimsical depictions of everyday life. His reputation was well-established. All he needed was an environment in which he could give free rein to his imagination.

The colonial house that he made his home—an eighteenth-century clapboard building—is now a warm and cozy bed-and-breakfast inn, very much as one imagines it might have been when Rockwell lived there.

Everything at the Inn on Covered Bridge Green is evocative of Rockwell's illustrations: the snug drawing room with its deep, inviting sofas, where the family gathered round the fire to leaf through the latest magazines; the dining room, reminiscent of his illustration of a traditional mealtime with a bunch of boisterous children seated at table, eagerly awaiting their hamburgers; eclectic collections of objects and books of all sorts on the shelves, just as in his domestic interiors; an armchair strewn with

plump cushions to make a quiet corner for reading; and little old tables on which you can just imagine protesting children doing their homework.

Rockwell's studio, now also part of the inn, was a separate little red cabin in the garden, and beside it the inevitable wooden couch hammock. With its period furniture and soft colors, the room he slept in, now known as "Spooners," is charming, as are all the other bedrooms. You can almost see him here, welcoming the friends and neighbors he loved to draw, showing them the magazine covers on which they appeared, seen throughout the world.

Rockwell spent his most prolific years here. It was in Arlington that he found the strongest expression of his inimitable style, his tender, gently humorous way of painting the people around him, their trades and pastimes, and moments of intimacy and emotion that speak to people of all nations. And Rockwell recognized that Arlington had boosted his career, offering him the opportunity to live in a world that was, he used to say, "more honest, in a way."

His works are like painted stories, each with its own fully developed narrative. Every meticulously

The colonial facade of the Inn on Covered Bridge Green, former home of Norman Rockwell.

Norman Rockwell with his dogs in Vermont, ca. 1950s; each room in the hotel has its own private fireplace. Opposite: A red covered bridge near Arlington.

A bed-and-breakfast inn in the Vermont house that was once the home of the illustrator Norman Rockwell is as elegant, refreshing, and authentic in spirit as his paintings.

detailed setting pinpoints his subject more accurately than words, as he whisks us off on exhilarating whistle-stop tours—by car, train, or plane—to café counters, art galleries, and doctors' waiting rooms; to ice-cream parlors, the top of the Statue of Liberty, or a riverside fishing trip. Over fourteen years he painted some two hundred inhabitants of Arlington, who, thanks to him, gained a certain celebrity. Some of them still live here, and are happy to give talks, sign autographs, and answer visitors' questions.

Some four hours' drive from New York, these real backdrops to Rockwell's imaginary world were there to be discovered: the old houses and farms of Arlington, lovely and unpretentious; the people on its streets; its discreet wooden signs. With the archetypal general stores, selling clothes for farm workers alongside household goods, they conjure up familiar images and an evocative sense of déjà-vu. Charming in its simplicity, the town is also extremely elegant, with its antique

THE SATURDAY EVENING

POST

NOVEMBER 18, 1950   15¢

**THE BIG URANIUM RUSH
OF 1950**
By John Bartlow Martin

Is the Marshall Plan Dead?
By Demaree Bess

Rockwell's studio, a separate cabin on the property. Opposite (clockwise from top):
Norman Rockwell at work in the 1940s; the interior of a guest room at the hotel;
the *Saturday Evening Post* cover featuring *Boy Practicing Trumpet* from November 1950.

shops, cottages, and whitewashed churches. In the fall (when everything is at its most beautiful), the structures are framed by foliage in dazzling cadences of scarlet and ochre, yellow and gold, forming multicolored drifts among the covered bridges, ponds, lakes, and rivers that punctuate this bucolic landscape. Visitors can't help feeling delighted to discover a place like this, where the spirit of the early settlers lives on, authentic and refreshing—just like Rockwell's drawings.

THE LENOX

Enrico Caruso

The year is 1907. Enrico Caruso, the Neapolitan tenor who has just dazzled his adoring fans in San Francisco, Oakland, and New York, arrives at the Lenox in his private train, accompanied—according to a report in the *New York Times*—by his secretary and three detectives (or as we would call them, bodyguards), declaring: "My previous visits to Boston have always been delightful. I always enjoy myself in Boston." The Lenox was the natural choice for his stay. Opened in 1900 by Lucius Boomer, owner of the Waldorf-Astoria, this was the most luxurious hotel in New England, with a refined ambience worthy of the most palatial European grand hotel. With its facade of red-and-white brick, its eleven stories, its lounges of unparalleled elegance and its enviable position on the corner of Boylston and Exeter in the heart of the Back Bay, a stone's throw from the exclusive shops on Newbury Street, The Lenox made all the front pages. This was the place to see and be seen.

At the time of his visit, Caruso was the most famous opera singer in the world. A legendary performer and undisputed star, he toured

A moonlit view of Faneuil Hall Marketplace.

The famous tenor Enrico Caruso and his wife, Dorothy. Opposite: The entrance to
The Lenox. Caruso is said to have arrived at the hotel in his private railroad car.

America coast to coast, singing "Amor ti vieta," his most popular hit, countless times and giving triumphant performances wherever he went. The American concerts marked the apogee of his fame. At The Lenox he is reputed to have delighted guests by giving an impromptu demonstration of his talents in the middle of the hotel lobby. Picture the scene, as—without even stopping to take off his traveling coat or hat, without putting down his cane, but always secretly clutching the good-luck charm that never left him—the illustrious tenor launched into an a capella rendition of "O Sole Mio."

Since that time, other musicians, such as Tony Bennett and Blondie, have taken the place of the great Caruso, and a district that was once just marshland has seen luxury restaurants and architectural treasures spring up, as well as magnificent nineteenth-century residences and futuristic constructions such as I. M. Pei's John Hancock Tower. This sixty-story building is now (as the Lenox once was) the tallest in Boston, the city that claims a special place as the cradle of American independence, and that is now so cosmopolitan, with so many different faces. The Lenox, designated a historic hotel of America, remains the ultrachic destination that it always was, attracting guests of wealth and fame from the world over. Regular visitors value the friendliness of the staff and the handsome rooms, classic in style, some with open fireplaces, and all imbued with the timeless charm of a true institution. Crystal chandeliers, dark wood furniture, Italian marble bathrooms, and lofty ceilings, and a long, splendid history lend this hotel a special cachet. But this is also a hotel on a

The famed venue the City Bar at The Lenox.
Opposite: Enrico Caruso, ca. 1918.

human scale, recently refurbished, where you feel at home as soon as you arrive.

My room looked out over Boylston Street—next to Newbury Street, one of the liveliest in the city—so evocatively described by Henry James in *The Bostonians*. From the hotel, the visitor can stroll to the public gardens and Trinity Church, and explore the narrow cobbled streets of old Boston, with its unexpected little passageways still lit by gas lamps. In the Beacon Hill district, with its secluded and perfectly tended little gardens, brick sidewalks and nineteenth-century town houses, quiet corners and village atmosphere, you could almost think you were in London's leafy Belgravia or Notting Hill. Boston should be explored on foot, if possible, at a leisurely pace that allows you to discover the treasures concealed between its skyscrapers, and which lend the city its aristocratic air. And opera fans will be delighted to learn that the hotel concierge will happily supply seats for performances of the Boston Lyric Opera, in the city's historic heart.

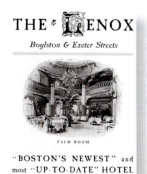

VOLCANO HOUSE
Mark Twain

The brazen cheek of Tom Sawyer augured well. Any writer who could invent such a character—rebellious, resourceful, free as the air—had to be a force to be reckoned with himself. And indeed Mark Twain was as unpredictable as his hero. His life took many surprising twists, including becoming a a steamboat pilot on the Mississippi, working as a reporter in Virginia City, and setting off on tours of California and Nevada to do readings of his memoirs. It was impossible to pin this mercurial writer down.

It was a virtually unknown journalist by the name of Samuel Clemens—Twain's real name—who arrived in Hawaii in 1866. He had come to write an article for the *Sacramento Union,* which had sent him to the Hawaiian islands, as well as to France and Italy. This was the journey that was to earn Twain his spurs as a writer. Nobody at the time believed for a moment that he genuinely undertook the journeys he described—an attitude of scant respect that was to enable the newspaper, when it hit hard times, to raise a princely sum by selling an old table off as "the desk at which Twain sat."

When Twain arrived in Honolulu, in March of 1866, he intended to stay for a month. As it turned out, he stayed for six months, writing stories and letters. In June, he traveled to see the Kilauea volcano. There he stayed in the Volcano House, a simple wooden, grass-thatched building with a parlor, fireplace, dining room, and four bedrooms. The first evening, he ate a "hearty supper" and waited for night to fall before setting out for the immense crater so that he could observe the volcanic activity in the darkness. "The first glance in that direction revealed a scene of wild beauty," he later recounted in *Roughing It.* "You could imagine those lights the width of a continent away . . . and even then the tremendous vista stretched on, and on and on!—to the fires and beyond! You could not compass it—it was the idea of eternity made tangible—and the longest end of it made visible to the naked eye!"

Writing to a friend in California, Twain described the hotel as "neat, roomy, well furnished and well kept," and commented that "the surprise of finding a good hotel at such an outlandish spot startled me considerably more than the volcano

Volcano House sits at the edge of Kilauea Crater.

A portrait of Mark Twain; a view off the coast of Hawaii.
Opposite: Plumeria in Hawaii.

> **" A colossal column of cloud towered to a great height in the air immediately above the crater, and the outer swell of every one of its vast folds was dyed with a rich crimson luster … It glowed like a muffled torch and stretched upward to a dizzy height toward the zenith. "**

did." Robert Louis Stevenson, Jack London, and Herman Melville shared his fascination with these islands, and the Volcano House continued to welcome guests from all over the world. Lying within the Hawai'i Volcanoes National Park on the Big Island, the hotel allows visitors to approach the massive Kilauea crater from the southeast, where the rim rises to four thousand feet above sea level. In addition to its spectacular volcanic activity, hiking trails, and wilderness, a rainforest with exotic flora and fauna makes the park an unmissable experience.

The small wooden building in which Mark Twain stayed has been considerably enlarged and modernized since 1866. But it is still the only hotel

The Volcano House fireplace; the hotel was built in the Ohia forest in 1846.
Opposite: The Ka Ohelo Dining Room looks out onto the spectacular Kilauea Caldera and Halemaumau Crater.

in Volcanoes National Park, and it has retained its simple, friendly atmosphere, boasting that the welcoming fire in its lobby has burned bright for over one hundred and twenty-five years. The main house has been rebuilt to offer twenty-four rooms, all with Hawaiian koa wood furnishings; some rooms enjoy views of the crater, others overlook the garden. The hotel also has the only restaurant in the park and a small shop, and it offers guided walks to view the volcano, experience the rainforest, discover the local wildlife, and witness the spectacle of fountains of lava shooting up over three hundred feet.

It was a sight that left Twain awestruck: "A colossal column of cloud towered to a great height in the air immediately above the crater, and the outer swell of every one of its vast folds was dyed with a rich crimson luster . . . It glowed like a muffled torch and stretched upward to a dizzy height toward the zenith." He also wrote, "Here and there were gleaming holes a hundred feet in diameter, broken in the dark crust, and in them the melted lava . . . was boiling and surging furiously; and from these holes branched numberless light torrents in many directions, like the spokes of a wheel . . . then swept round in huge rainbow curves."

SAN YSIDRO RANCH

Jacqueline and John F. Kennedy

In 1953, John and Jackie Kennedy arrived at San Ysidro Ranch, a Rosewood Resort, to spend part of their honeymoon. Both of them knew what awaited them. Jackie had been warned that men in the Kennedy clan were womanizers, that they thought they could invent their own rules and imagined they were above all laws. John knew Jackie was the woman for him. "I don't want to marry a girl who is an experienced voyageur," he said, "and I'm not referring to travel." Jackie had been to Europe and had been brought up with the idea that she must marry a wealthy man. John was rich, ambitious, and had just been elected to represent Massachusetts in Congress. He needed an elegant, aristocratic wife, who was Catholic like himself, to propel him to the top. Both families thought the match was perfect, as they had gone through all other possibilities with a fine-toothed comb. Jackie and John were married on September 12, 1953. More than three thousand people waited feverishly for the arrival of the limousine in front of Saint Mary's Church in Newport. Around thirteen hundred guests were at the party given at Hammersmith Farm, on Rhode Island. John's father had already sold the photos in advance to the *New York Times* and the *Boston Globe*. Everything had been planned to make the best impression in front of the press and their guests. After New York and the Acapulco beaches, the young newlyweds rejoined in California and checked in for a week in what is today Kennedy Cottage, a delightful bungalow nestled in the middle of oak trees and bougainvillea, surrounded by acres of wonderful gardens and hills. The golden couple took as much advantage as possible of their stay. They visited friends in Monterey, the seaside resort dear to John Steinbeck, some one hundred and eighty miles to the north. John went to a football match one day with his friend Red Fay, while Jackie and Fay's wife took advantage of this time to visit Marin County and its nearby vineyards. From the terrace of their bungalow they could see the other cottages dispersed between the jasmine and the eucalyptus and admire the blue hills of Santa Ynez. It's impossible to imagine more superb gardens, except perhaps for those of the White House. (They got there seven years later.)

Santa Barbara is a splendid colonial village ninety miles from Los Angeles on the Pacific Coast

Through the doors of a private suite on San Ysidro Ranch lie the rolling hills of Santa Barbara's wine country.

The Kennedy Cottage bedroom.

Highway, well-known to all those who are seeking peace and quiet in the sun. Built in the eighteenth century on the site of the ancestral home of the Chumash Indians, Santa Barbara has retained traces of its Spanish past, with its adobe houses, pretty, narrow streets, and arcade-lined squares. No skyscrapers, no unsightly buildings. Spanish-style tiles decorate mail boxes, street signs, and

Clockwise from top: John and Jackie in 1953; the exterior of the cottage, where the newlywed Kennedy couple stayed; the swimming pool and lounge chairs at San Ysidro in the 1950s.

telephone booths, and a McDonald's there is even done in adobe! Life takes place outside, on café terraces, restaurant patios, and around State and El Paso streets, the typical shopping mall opposite the town hall. You can visit the old Santa Barbara mission at the end of Laguna Street, the most important Franciscan mission in California, where twenty-five brothers still live today, and in

The entrance sign to San Ysidro Ranch; John and Jackie in 1953; A view of San Ysidro with the ocean in the background.

Deliciously Californian, San Ysidro Ranch is the secluded hideaway of the stars. Wonderful weather and stunning bungalows nestled among orange and eucalyptus trees, with all the charm of Santa Barbara only a few minutes away.

March and April you can board one of the boats which leave the port every day to see the incredible sight of gray whales swimming in the open seas on their way toward warmer waters. The district of Montecito is set back a little farther away from the town and for a long time, the land on which the San Ysidro Ranch stands was home only to orange and lemon groves. Indeed, it was only after the 1930s, when the actor Ronald Colman and the hotel owner Alvin Carl Weingand purchased the place, that the San Ysidro Ranch's name started to circulate in Hollywood, attracting stars seeking a relaxed, romantic sanctuary only an hour away—by limousine—from Los Angeles. The San Ysidro

Ranch is very definitely relaxed, but with elegance, charm, and opulence, affording the sort of secluded informality glamorous couples favor. On arrival, one is pleasantly surprised to discover one's name engraved on a small wooden sign near the door. Guests can spend their days on the golf course or in the swimming pool, and in the evenings, quietly enjoy a glass of champagne or Chardonnay—the region of the Californian vineyards is not far away—in jeans and sneakers. This stunning five hundred-acre ranch overlooks the Pacific Ocean and the Channel Islands and, as a result of its unrivaled geographic position between sea and mountains, enjoys the most wonderful climate. Vivien Leigh and Laurence Olivier were married in the gardens of the San Ysidro. Natalie Wood, Fred Astaire, Gloria Swanson, Jean Harlow, Audrey Hepburn, and David Niven, among others, sought shelter in this luxurious hideaway amid orange trees and jasmine. And John Huston completed the screenplay for *The African Queen* here—yet another story of a great couple.

POST RANCH INN

Jack Kerouac

In the summer of 1960 Jack Kerouac arrived at Big Sur—the isolated region south of the Bay Area that had become a refuge for hermits of all descriptions—determined to forget everything. He had had enough of living up to the image of the crazy road-tripper of *On the Road*; of being hunted down by the press, his fans, the spongers, and the merely curious; of playing the part, like an obedient puppet, of "king of the Beats." Success was the worst thing that could have happened to him. Depressed and embittered by his years of rejection (written in 1948, *On the Road* was not published until 1957), he spent his days drinking in order to forget that he had turned into everything that he hated most. He still published books, but they were books written before he was successful and attracted little interest. He appeared on television, but often canceled interviews; when he did go through with them, journalists often found him arrogant and incoherent.

It was on the advice of his friend the poet Lawrence Ferlinghetti, who had rented a cabin at Bixby Canyon, that Kerouac traveled to Big Sur on the Pacific coast, to a semblance of a village between Malpaso Creek and the Salinas Valley, utterly lost in the wilderness. With its rocky creeks, forests of sequoias contorted by the wind and isolated cabins clinging to cliff faces, it was a strange region that appealed to bohemian spirits, artists and lovers of wild, rugged landscapes and freedom. Kerouac's time here was not to bring him the tranquility he yearned for. Far from it: he rapidly took a violent dislike to the place, and his mental state deteriorated. Terrified by untamed nature and the forest noises around him, he was convinced on one occasion that he saw flying saucers, and angels on another. Often he woke in the middle of the night moaning, the bottle never far away. One night he suffered an attack of delirium tremens, his hands shaking so violently that he couldn't light a cigarette. By day he panicked for no reason, refused to meet Henry Miller, who lived nearby, managing only to drag himself to the Nepenthe restaurant on Highway One to down a string of Manhattans. His new book came out of this adventure of teetering on the brink of madness. *Big Sur,* the story of a final quest fueled by alcohol and Benzedrine, was another desperate,

The coastline in Big Sur.

Clockwise from above: The hotel's award-winning restaurant Sierra Mar, resting on a cliff above Big Sur; the meditative infinity pool with the Pacific Ocean as a backdrop; a table with a view at the hotel's restaurant; the Peak House on the east side of the property has a captivating view; Kerouac, Lucien Carr, and Allen Ginsberg in 1959.

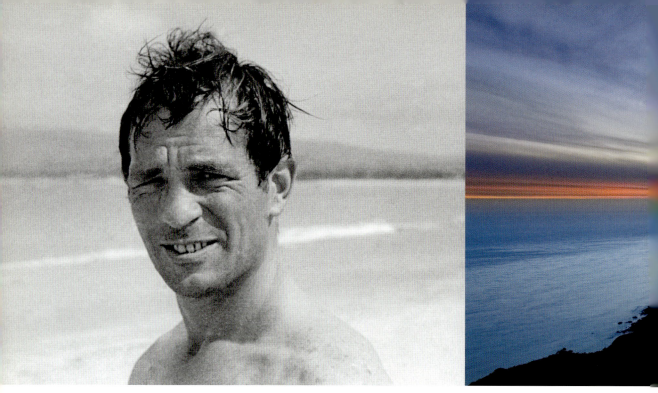

Jack Kerouac on the beach, ca. 1957. Kerouac escaped Long Island, New York, hoping to find refuge along the California coastline at Big Sur; the deck of the Pacific Suite.

*Breathtaking Californian
landscapes and seascapes, individual houses
hidden in the forest, a haven of
organic luxury amid the majesty of nature.*

hallucinatory cry for help, erupting from a cabin lost in the wilderness. Kerouac ended it with a poem about the "voices" of the Pacific Ocean that harried him, as peace still eluded him.

Big Sur packs a strong punch. This is not a place for those of a vulnerable disposition, or with a sentimental love of sweet, bucolic landscapes. Big Sur is weird, extreme, tortured, fascinating, bizarre, mind-blowing. Big Sur is for lovers of strange places, of solitude, bracing air, landscapes untouched by human hand and worlds apart; for

lovers of the writing of Steinbeck, who lived close by at Monterey. From Post Ranch Inn, the beauties of this region hit you between the eyes. Perched up high in solitary splendor, the hotel and its astonishing little single-room houses in the forest look out into the mountains or down onto the coastline below. This is the perfect spot for a honeymoon, or for the dream of freedom for which Kerouac hoped. It is also a magnificent enclave of rustic luxury, where every element—wood, glass, and stone, ringed by giant trees and wooded hills—is

simple and beautiful. Close by are the beaches of Carmel, the famous 17-Mile Drive and the Point Lobos State Reserve, another pristine sanctuary, where you can see condors, southern sea otters, and harbor seals barking on the rocks. As you follow the discreetly designated trails, dazzled by the majesty of this "greatest meeting of land and water in the world," you can't help marveling that it has been possible to preserve all this beauty in its unspoilt, virgin state.

Post Ranch Inn dates from 1867. Twenty years earlier, an eighteen-year-old Yankee pioneer, William Brainard Post, had stepped off a ship at Mon-

terey, his head full of dreams and plans. From the cattle ranch he established in 1850, the Post family gradually created a magnificent hotel, with individual wooden cabins in the woods, self-contained independent houses, and tree houses perched in majestic boughs. With its organic, sustainable architecture, the hotel looks as if it has grown out of the surrounding forest. Kerouac didn't manage to conquer his demons here, but in this unique spot it's not hard to understand why Big Sur and the surrounding region still enjoy a quasi-mythical reputation among artists, intellectuals, eccentrics, and outsiders, whether famous or not.

MABEL DODGE LUHAN HOUSE

D. H. Lawrence

If you tend by nature to be pragmatic, rational and logical, or straightforward and structured in your habits of thought, then heed this advice: Taos is not for you. Taos is for those who believe anything is possible, way beyond established codes and carefully modulated forms of happiness. This enclave of New Mexico, which joined the Union only in 1912, is a heady mix of Native American and Hispanic influences, spirits, and storytellers, a place that exalts in creativity, originality and a bohemian lifestyle, where the quality of the light would be enough in itself to make you want to stay here for the rest of your life.

D. H. Lawrence came to New Mexico in September of 1922, at the invitation of Mabel Dodge Luhan, a prominent patron of the arts and an artist herself. This passionate devotee of the arts settled at Taos in 1919 after spending periods in Europe, notably at her Medici villa outside Florence, Villa Curonia, where she welcomed a throng of artists. Along with attempting to persuade Lawrence that his genius would be perfectly at home in the atmo-

sphere at Taos (even enclosing some Native American herbs), Mabel wrote him to say she would put the house at his disposal, along with everything he would need to work. Lawrence wrote back immediately, anxious to ascertain that the place would not be filled with pseudo-artists; once reassured on this point, he accepted Mabel's offer. When he arrived with his wife, Frieda, Mabel was waiting for them at the train station in her Cadillac. She invited other artists and intellectuals, including Carl Jung, Willa Cather, and Ansel Adams, but the Lawrences were the only ones to stay (on and off) for such a lengthy period—from 1922 to 1925.

Mabel's property at this time consisted of a corral, five guesthouses—including the Pink House, specially built for the Lawrences—and staff quarters. Taos boasted a population of some two thousand, a dusty plaza, and a few other houses. The atmosphere was bizarre, with magical overtones that were a gift for a writer.

Mabel and Frieda were close in age, and both were apostles of free love, and ultimately this was

Many great minds of the 20th century have stayed at the Mabel Dodge Luhan House.

Above (clockwise from top): A guest room; a portrait of D. H. Lawrence; American author Mabel Dodge Luhan. Opposite: Lawrence and his wife, Frieda, ca. 1920s.

an adventure that was doomed to crumble amid jealous tantrums and lost ideals. Nonetheless, in later years, Lawrence claimed that Taos had been the greatest experience of his life. "It changed me forever," he said. He would use his time in New Mexico as inspiration for his novel *The Plumed Serpent,* while Mabel produced a volume of memoirs of this period entitled *Lorenzo in Taos.*

In the intervening period, the Mabel Dodge Luhan House has been transformed into a hotel that

can boast among its guests an array of artists, poets, thinkers, and musicians who have come here in search of an ideal refuge, including Georgia O'Keeffe, Gustave Baumann, Mary Austin, Albert Cohen, Bob Dylan, and Dennis Hopper. Behind the sturdy gates, the adobe house at the foot of the mountains continues to live the legend, with its art studios, its windows painted by D. H. Lawrence, its rooms paying tribute to famous visitors, its flower-filled terrace, and its cool, private corners. Mabel's

The energy in Taos is mystical, historical, and inspiring to artists, writers, and thinkers even today. Opposite: a traditional adobe structure in Taos Pueblo.

room is still here, with its spectacular view of the mountains. Georgia O'Keeffe's room, on the first floor, is smaller and more intimate. The room used by Ansel Adams, and later Dennis Hopper, opens onto to a pretty little terrace shared with another room. The room where Willa Cather wrote overlooks the main courtyard. The windows painted by D. H. Lawrence are in the solarium, where visitors can take in the glories of the surrounding landscape in a single sweeping glance. And yes, there is an energy, a freedom, a spirituality even, pushing you forward and giving inspiration, coming from who knows where? Perhaps from the wide-open spaces you cross to reach here; perhaps from the ruined pueblos and haciendas that dot the region, surviving in spite of everything; or perhaps from that particular mix of the Hispanic and Native American spirit, combined with the many artists who have left their mark here, together endowing the tiniest moments with that special feeling unique to Taos.

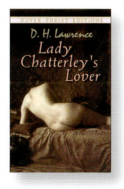

CHATEAU MARMONT
Jim Morrison

I love Chateau Marmont above all for the stories that haunt and sustain it, for the ghosts and dreams that inhabit it, for its moments of madness and its flamboyant extravagance. Because it was built on the model of a chateau of the Loire Valley, because it out-Hollywoods Hollywood, because it hovers somewhere between being cool and trashy, and because since 1929 it has always been there, on the heights of Sunset Boulevard, and because people always write about it.

Montgomery Clift convalesced here after the accident that nearly killed him. Jean Harlow and Clark Gable conducted a torrid affair here. Led Zeppelin roared through the lobby on their Harley Davidsons. All Hollywood royalty has stayed here, including James Dean and Humphrey Bogart, along with iconic musicians of yesterday and today—Gram Parsons, Jefferson Airplane, Frank Zappa . . .

From 1970 to 1971, one James Douglas Morrison lived here: Jim Morrison, the "Lizard King," poet, outsider and, incidentally, front man and lead singer for The Doors. A lot had changed since the band's dazzling debut in 1967, and Morrison was but a shadow of the glorious sex symbol he had so

recently been—depressed, chain-smoking, downing one beer after another, and overweight. The striking change in his physical appearance was further accentuated by the bushy beard he had grown. The band, which had just brought out what was to be their last real album, *L.A. Woman,* was in a similarly sorry state. Within a few months, Morrison would leave the band and move to Paris—where, in July of 1971, he died. Away from the spotlight of publicity, Morrison divided his time during those last years between hotels in Los Angeles and the Laurel Canyon apartment of his girlfriend, Pamela Courson. He checked in to the Chateau Marmont the way other people might go to stay with their grandmother, but this stay was to signal the end to his nomadic L.A. lifestyle. One night, drunk as usual, he attempted to get into his room by jumping through the window from the hotel roof. The ensuing fall broke two of his ribs, and he said that the incident had used up the eighth of his nine lives.

If hotels take on the image of the tales that are woven around them, the Chateau Marmont is no exception. Nostalgia and illusion, decadence and delusion mingle here in a heady cocktail,

The Chateau Marmont is enclosed by trees and flowering vines.

The entrance to the hotel's Garden Cottage.
Opposite: Jim Morrison, ca. 1970.

Sex, fun, and rock 'n' roll. A jaw-dropping history,
a list of famous guests, film idols, and
rock stars that goes on forever, a gilded promise of
eternal youth and glamour ...

and the cathedral-like vaulted ceilings have been witness to a delirious mix of glamour, scandal, and wild excesses.

Hidden around a bend on Sunset Boulevard, when it finally appears, the hotel looks deserted. Inside, the dark furniture has the air of having lived many lives, the floorboards creak. The atmosphere is intimate, bohemian, part Gothic, part Spanish, with the occasional dash of contemporary style. The lobby, surprisingly silent on each of my visits, has an instantly familiar feel, with low velvet sofas, a little writing table, magazines in a corner. Light filters in from the garden, and the view of trees and greenery, framed by the Gothic window gives the feeling of a medieval painting.

The bungalows are like miniature country houses engulfed in greenery. The secluded atmosphere is conducive to secrets and confidences. Most of the sixty or so suites, cottages and bungalows

Clockwise from above: a secluded entrance to one of the Marmont bungalows; interior of one of the guestrooms; view of the pool from the roof of the hotel.

The terrace of the two-bedroom Penthouse Suite.

have their own kitchens, dining rooms and terraces. Guests can throw dinners and parties, welcome whomever they like however they like, relive old times. The swimming pool is also surrounded by gardens, and clients flock to the bar throughout the year. What I like best is sitting at one of the patio tables for a drink or having dinner with friends. Or simply sitting outside, beneath the Gothic arches, and breathing in the L.A. air.

Fashionable hotels are legion, but when you see furniture that seems to have experienced more than its fair share of life, the pale light of dawn signaling that the party is not over yet, the fantastical surroundings of a medieval manor house, and clients who seem to have spent several nights without sleep, you know you are at the Chateau Marmont and nowhere else.

MAISON DE VILLE

Tennessee Williams

I don't know of any city that is more be-witching than New Orleans, which is hardly surprising since voodoo practice is inextri-cably linked with its history. The streets are still filled with the rhythm of the blues sung by slaves on the plantations. The churches and chapels swell with full-throated gospel singing. With its matchless heritage—Creole and Cajun, Satchmo and swing, Jean Lafitte the buccaneer and Tennessee Williams and his streetcar—this is a city that is able to endure the worst, live through the darkest hours, and still remain as captivating and ir-resistible as it ever was.

So Tennessee Williams must have thought, too, as he downed one Sazerac—the cocktail of choice here—after another in his room at the Hotel Maison de Ville. It was 1939, and he had just turned his back on his puritanical family in order to live a nomad-ic life in the heart of the French Quarter. Moving from hotel to apartment and back to hotel, as doors opened and closed again, he changed hotel rooms as often as he changed

The lush courtyard of the Maison de Ville.

The Preservation Jazz Band playing in the French Quarter in 1995;
Williams, ca. 1970; an accordionist playing on Bourbon Street.

> ❝ *In the heart of the French Quarter,*
> *a residence of some twenty rooms of colonial charm*
> *telling the whole story of New Orleans.* ❞

partners. His hotel rooms spanned the globe, a heteroclite collection that formed the central thread to a life that would reach its dramatic end in a hotel room (where else?) in New York. In New Orleans, the French Quarter—and Toulouse Street in particular—was to offer him a rich and inexhaustible source of observation and inspiration. His memories of people he met in New Orleans would inspire the characters in his plays, and many years later he made a pilgrimage back here. He kept his apartment close to the hotel to the end of his life.

His room at the Hotel Maison de Ville, Room 9, opens onto a private patio surrounded by tropical plants and flowers. This is where he wrote, downing Sazeracs all the while, preferably in the quiet atmosphere of the patio—sheltering, tranquil, bohemian. It was in this room, which now bears his name, that he finished writing *A Streetcar Named Desire.* Did he rise at dawn to write here, as he did when he lived in another hotel room in Tangiers? Did he go and read the newspapers on nearby Bourbon Street, or did he follow his old habits and go to the corner

café? Did he spend his afternoons strolling the French Quarter and drinking with friends and acquaintances? More than likely he did, since he was a regular at the Hotel Monteleone's Carousel Bar—along with other distinguished barflies, including Truman Capote, Ernest Hemingway, and William Faulkner.

A true Southern establishment, imbued with poetry and Creole charm, the Hotel Maison de Ville has extended hospitality to travelers for generations, and is reputed to be haunted by the spirits of some of those who have passed through during its two-hundred-plus years of history, including the slaves who used to have quarters here. Discreet and private, it is burnished and worn with a patina of age that makes it even more moving.

Many of the rooms are arranged around the cool courtyard with its fountain. Then there are separate cottages, an unexpected pool—the oldest in the French Quarter—and a bistro serving frogs' legs, just like in Paris. As always in New Orleans, there is a legend for every room. One inspired the naturalist John James Audubon, who painted many of his *Birds of America* here. Another received Elizabeth Taylor. Another is haunted, so they say. And the hotel boasts several ghosts who are "regulars," eternal guests forever in residence.

Affecting and with more than a touch of mystery about it, this is a hotel that breathes authenticity and character. As you walk out onto Toulouse Street after spending a little time here, you feel that you are already part of the city—in a way. I can see it all now: the narrow streets, the magnificent courtyards glimpsed through half-open carriage entrances, the glorious profusion of wrought-iron balconies. I can still smell the aromas of Creole cooking, of the vegetation in the heavy, humid hothouse atmosphere, of Café Brûlot with its spices flamed in rum. And in the midst of it all, barely discernible, just a hint of the wicked absinthe notes of a perfectly chilled glass of Sazerac.

Clockwise from above: The hotel pool; the hotel exterior; Williams at his typewriter in 1956.

The playwright preferred Room 9, and so it was named "The Tennessee Williams Room."

FAIRMONT HOTEL
Vertigo

The Fairmont San Francisco has a history every bit as terrifying as a Hitchcock film. On April 18, 1906, when work on the building was nearly finished, an earthquake measuring 8.5 on the Richter scale devastated the city. Buildings collapsed and gas mains ruptured, causing an immense conflagration that raged for two days. The Fairmont, symbol of the city's pride and dynamism, was engulfed in flames and looked as if it would be completely destroyed. Although the structure did in fact survive, the interior was ruined. Months of frenetic work would be needed to restore it to its former glory. Finally, and miraculously, it opened the following year. After such a harrowing beginning, the hotel was ready to receive its guests—notably among them, years later, the "master of suspense."

When he arrived at the hotel, in 1957, Alfred Hitchcock was fifty-eight years old and had made more than forty films. He had decided to film *Vertigo* in San Francisco, which he called "the Paris of America," supposedly

The front entrance of The Fairmont.

A still from the 1959 film; the Penthouse Suite's wraparound balcony offers views of the bay city's skyline and Golden Gate Bridge; Kim Novak and James Stewart on the set of *Vertigo*.

Part of San Francisco's history since 1906, mingling a long, nostalgic history with European charm, The Fairmont's luxury and classic elegance seduced the 'master of suspense'.

choosing the locations first, and then working the plot around them. San Francisco, a city with a European air that could conceal all sorts of mysteries, seemed to him a peculiarly appropriate setting for a psychological thriller. Impressed by the French novel *D'entre les morts (From Among the Dead)* by Pierre Boileau and Thomas Narcejac, Hitchcock decided to bring the story and the city together. Substituting San Francisco for Paris and changing the end of the novel, he embarked on

filming what was to be another of his trademark thrillers, but above all an astonishingly modern film for its time, making full use of San Francisco and its urban landscapes.

Hitchcock set the apartment of Madeleine (Kim Novak) in the Brocklebank, an apartment block at 1000 Mason Street (just opposite the Fairmont), which has hardly changed in the intervening years, and where the Pulitzer Prize–winning journalist Herb Caen lived. As Hitchcock—like Marlene Dietrich, Ella Fitzgerald, and Nat King Cole—habitually stayed at The Fairmont when he was in San Francisco, the hotel was the obvious place to set up his headquarters during filming. The hotel concierge, Tom Wolfe, still remembers this time—though curiously he only met Hitchcock on one occasion—and especially remembers hearing Kim Novak's unmistakable voice over the telephone.

Eleven years before *Bullitt* and its legendary car chase, Hitchcock made San Francisco a ubiquitous presence in film, with locations including Mission Dolores, the Palace of the Legion of Honor, Golden Gate Bridge, Cypress Point on 17 Mile Drive near Pebble Beach, and the apartment of Scottie (James Stewart), at 900 Lombard Street.

It was in the Venetian Room at The Fairmont—meeting place of choice for San Francisco residents since the 1940s—that Tony Bennett first sang "I Left My Heart in San Francisco." Another celebrated space is the astonishing Cirque Room, decorated by the architect Tim Pflueger in pure

Stewart and Novak on set; the Penthouse Suite.
Opposite: The ceiling of the hotel's two-story library depicts the constellations of the nighttime sky.

Art Deco style, with frescoes by the Bolivian artist Antonio Sotomayor. The first bar to open in the post-Prohibition era, this was always the place to be seen.

And then there is the famous Penthouse Suite, with its spectacular views over the city, which has become as much the stuff of legend as the stories that surround it. Built as a private residence in 1926, it occupies the entire floor, with three bedrooms, four bathrooms, a dining room seating up to fifty guests, a magnificent oval library, four fireplaces and a billiard room. Who has stayed here? Who hasn't? And film buffs will recognize the suite that Sean Connery's character demands in the 1996 film *The Rock*—his ultimate dream on his release from Alcatraz—and where (on the terrace) he receives a particularly memorable haircut.

LEGENDARY
HOTELS
of the United States

Create your own legend at one of the notable hotels across the United States in Assouline's guide to stylish Mountain, Beach, Country, and City destinations.

The Sunset Tower in Los Angeles at dusk.

MOUNTAIN

ALASKA

Pearson's Pond Luxury Inn
Juneau
Tel: 888.658.6328
www.pearsonspond.com

COLORADO

The Home Ranch
Clark
Tel: 970.879.1780
www.homeranch.com

Hotel Jerome
Aspen
Tel: 877.412.7625
www.hoteljerome.rockresorts.com

Hotel Lenado
Aspen
Tel: 800.321.3457
www.hotellenado.com

The Lodge
Vail
Tel: 877.528.7625
www.lodgeatvail.rockresorts.com

Mount Princeton Resort
Nathrop
Tel: 888.395.7799
www.mtprinceton.com

The Ritz-Carlton Bachelor Gulch
Avon
Tel: 970.748.6200
www.ritzcarlton.com

Sky Hotel
Aspen
Tel: 800.882.2582
www.theskyhotel.com

Sonnenalp Resort
Vail
Tel: 866.284.4411
www.sonnenalp.com

IDAHO

Knob Hill Inn
Ketchum
Tel: 800.526.8010
www.knobhillinn.com

MONTANA

Paws Up Resort
Greenough
Tel: 866.894.7969
www.pawsup.com

NEW YORK

Lake Placid Lodge
Lake Placid
Tel: 877.523.2700
www.lakeplacidlodge.com

Whiteface Lodge
Lake Placid
Tel: 800.903.4045
www.thewhitefacelodge.com

WYOMING

Amangani
Jackson
Tel: 877.734.7333
www.amangani.com

Snake River Lodge & Spa
Teton Village
Tel: 866.975.7625
www.snakeriverlodge.rockresorts.com

The Amangani in Jackson, Wyoming.

BEACH

CALIFORNIA

La Valencia
La Jolla
Tel: 800.451.0772
www.lavalencia.com

Oceana
Santa Monica
Tel: 800.777.0758
www.hoteloceanasantamonica.com

Shade Hotel
Manhattan Beach
Tel: 866.742.3377
www.shadehotel.com

Viceroy
Santa Monica
Tel: 800.670.6185
www.viceroysantamonica.com

OREGON

Tu Tu' Tun Lodge
Gold Beach
Tel: 800.864.6357
www.tututun.com

FLORIDA

The Betsy
Miami Beach
Tel: 866.531.9009
www.thebetsyhotel.com

The Delano
Miami Beach
Tel: 800.697.1791
www.delano-hotel.com

The Mondrian
Miami Beach
Tel: 800.697.1791
www.mondrian-miami.com

The Setai
South Beach
Tel: 888.625.7500
www.setai.com

The Shore Club
Miami Beach
Tel: 800.697.1791
www.shoreclub.com

The Standard
Miami Beach
Tel: 305.673.1717
www.standardhotels.com

The Tides
South Beach
Tel: 800.439.4095
www.tidessouthbeach.com

HAWAII

Halekulani Hotel
Honolulu
Tel: 800.367.2343
www.halekulani.com

Hotel Hana-Maui
Hana
Tel: 800.321.4262
www.hotelhanamaui.com

Kahala Hotel
Honolulu
Tel: 800.367.2525
www.kahalaresort.com

Kona Village Resort
Kailua-Kona
Tel: 800.367.5290
www.konavillage.com

The Penthouse Suite at the Shore Club in Miami Beach, Florida.

COUNTRY

ALASKA
Sadie Cove Wilderness Lodge
Homer
Tel: 888.283.7234

www.sadiecove.com

ARIZONA
Enchantment Resort
Sedona
Tel: 800.826.4180

www.enchantmentresort.com

CALIFORNIA
Auberge du Soleil
Napa Valley
Tel: 800.348.5406

www.aubergedusoleil.com

Solage
Calistoga
Tel: 866.942.7442

www.solagecalistoga.com

COLORADO
Dunton Hot Springs Resort
Dolores
Tel: 970.882.4800

www.duntonhotsprings.com

TENNESSEE
Blackberry Farm
Walland
Tel: 800.648.4252

www.blackberryfarm.com

TEXAS
The Thunderbird Hotel
Marfa
Tel: 432.729.1984

www.thunderbirdmarfa.com

MAINE
The Pentagöet Inn
Castine
Tel: 800.845.1701

www.pentagoet.com

MONTANA
Triple Creek Ranch
Darby
Tel: 800.654.2943

www.triplecreekranch.com

NEW HAMPSHIRE
The Manor on Golden Pond
Holderness
Tel: 800.545.2141

www.manorongoldenpond.com

NEW MEXICO
Hacienda de Cerezo
Santa Fe
Tel: 888.982.8001

www.haciendadelcerezo.com

Rancho de San Juan
Española
Tel: 505.753.6818

www.ranchodesanjuan.com

NEW YORK
The Point
Saranac Lake
Tel: 800.255.3530

www.thepointresort.com

VERMONT
Twin Farms Resort
Barnard
Tel: 800.894.6327

www.twinfarms.com

The outdoor patio of one the studios at Solage, in Calistoga, California.

CITY

The Standard in Los Angeles, California.
Following pages: The Ivy Hotel in San Diego, California.

CREDITS

All thumbnail-size hotel drawings, with the exception of the Chateau Marmont, were illustrated by Cyrene Mary and Miriam Hiersteiner. Page 4: © The Biltmore; p. 6: © Morgans Hotel Group; p. 9: © Ken Hayden, courtesy of The Raleigh Hotel; p. 10–11: © Nikolas Koenig, courtesy of The Raleigh Hotel (left), © Slim Aarons/Hulton Archive/Getty Images (center and right); p. 12: © Nikolas Koenig, courtesy of The Raleigh Hotel; p. 13: © Nikolas Koenig, courtesy of The Raleigh Hotel (top), courtesy of the Everett Collection (bottom); p. 15: Courtesy of Arizona Biltmore Resort & Spa; p. 16: © Marvin Koner/Corbis; p. 17: Courtesy of Arizona Biltmore Resort & Spa–Aztec Room; p. 18–19: © Marvin Koner/Corbis (left), courtesy of Arizona Biltmore–Adobe Golf Course (center), courtesy of Arizona Biltmore Resort & Spa–Wright's at the Biltmore Restaurant (right), © Viktoriya/Shutterstock (bottom); p. 21: © Theo Wargo/WireImage; p. 22–23: © Timothy A. Clary/AFP/Getty Images (left), © Pictorial Press Ltd./Alamy (center), © Corbis (right); p. 24: © Corbis (left), Cyrene Mary (right); p. 25: © Rue des Archives/The Granger Collection, New York; p. 27: Photo by Kelly Gorham Photography, courtesy of Rainbow Ranch Lodge; p. 28: Courtesy of Rainbow Ranch Lodge; p. 29: © Columbia Pictures, courtesy of the Everett Collection; p. 30–31: Photo by Larry Stanley, courtesy of Rainbow Ranch Lodge (left and center), photo by Kelly Gorham Photography, courtesy of Rainbow Ranch Lodge (right), © Columbia Pictures, courtesy of the Everett Collection (bottom); p. 33: Courtesy of The Breakers Palm Beach, all rights reserved; p. 34–35: Cover: detail from *Elizabeth Winthrop Chandler (Mrs. John Jay Chapman)*, 1893, by John Singer Sargent, courtesy of Penguin Press (left), courtesy of The Breakers Palm Beach, all rights reserved (center), courtesy of the Everett Collection (right); p. 36: Courtesy of The Breakers Palm Beach, all rights reserved; p. 37: © John Coletti/Getty Images (top), courtesy of the Library of America (bottom); p. 39: Courtesy of Colorado Trails Ranch; p. 40: © Dale O'Dell/Alamy; p. 41: Courtesy of Colorado Trails Ranch; p. 42: © Michael Ochs Archives/Corbis (top left), courtesy of Colorado Trails Ranch (top right and bottom); p. 43: Courtesy of Colorado Trails Ranch (top), courtesy of Colorado Trails Ranch, artwork © Pat Fullerton (bottom); p. 45: Courtesy of MGM Mirage; p. 46: © Warner Brothers, courtesy of the Everett Collection; p. 47: Courtesy of MGM Mirage; p. 48–49: Courtesy of MGM Mirage (top and bottom left), © Rue des Archives/BCA (bottom right); p. 51: © Andre Jenny/Alamy; p. 52–53: © Rob Howard/Corbis (left), © Bettmann/Corbis (center), courtesy of Sun Valley Resort (right); p. 54: © John Springer Collection/Corbis; p. 55: Courtesy Sun Valley Resort; p. 57, 58: Courtesy of the Hotel del Coronado; p. 59: © Ed Mari; p. 60: Courtesy of the Hotel del Coronado; p. 61: Courtesy of the Hotel del Coronado (top left, top right), Rue des Archives/BCA (bottom); p. 63: Courtesy of Don CeSar Beach Resort, A Loews Hotel; p. 64–65: © Nik Wheeler/Corbis (left), © Minnesota Historical Society/Corbis (center), courtesy of Don CeSar Beach Resort, A Loews Hotel (right); p. 66: © Bettmann/Corbis; p. 67: © Carl & Ann Purcell/Corbis (top), courtesy of Penguin Press UK (bottom); p. 69: Courtesy of The Carlyle, A Rosewood Hotel; p. 70: © Herbert Pfarrhofer/epa/Corbis (top), photo by Richard Termine, courtesy of The Carlyle (bottom left), *The Carlyle Hotel*, 1947, Museum of the City of New York, The Wurts Collection #817750 (bottom right); p. 71: Photo by Ed Masterson, courtesy of The Carlyle; p. 72, 73: Courtesy of The Carlyle, A Rosewood Hotel; p. 75: © PCL/Alamy; p. 76: Courtesy of the Everett Collection; p. 77: © Audrey Gibson/Corbis; p. 78: Courtesy of the Mission Ranch; p. 79: Courtesy of the Mission Ranch (top), Courtesy of the Everett Collection (bottom); p. 81: © The Biltmore; p. 82: © New York Times/Getty Images; p. 83, 84, 85: © The Biltmore; p. 87: Courtesy of the Sundance Resort; p. 88–89: Courtesy of Sundance Resort (top left), © Douglas Kirkland/Corbis (top right), © Bettmann/Corbis (bottom left), © John Springer Collection/Corbis (bottom right); p. 90: Courtesy of the Sundance Resort; p. 91: Courtesy of the Sundance Resort (top), © Jonathan Blair/Corbis (bottom); p. 93: © Clint Dickens/Inn on Covered Bridge Green; p. 94: © Buddy Mays/Corbis; p. 95: © Bettmann/Corbis (left), © Clint Dickens/Inn on Covered Bridge Green (right); p. 96: © Bettmann/Corbis (top), Printed by permission of the Norman Rockwell Family Agency, © 1950 SEPS: Licensed by Curtis Publishing, Indianapolis, IN, all rights reserved. www.curtispublishing.com (bottom), © Clint Dickens/Inn on Covered Bridge Green (bottom right); p. 97: © Clint Dickens/Inn on Covered Bridge Green (top), © Shutterstock (bottom); p. 99: © Atlantide Phototravel/Corbis; p. 100: © Hulton-Deutsch Collection/Corbis; p. 101: Courtesy of The Lenox Hotel; p. 102: © Bettmann/Corbis; p. 103: Courtesy of The Lenox Hotel (top), © Old Paper Studios/Alamy (bottom); p. 105: Courtesy of Volcano House; p. 106: © Macduff Everton/Corbis; p. 107: © Lebrecht Music and Arts Photo Library/Alamy (left), © RJN Fletcher/Alamy (right); p. 108: Courtesy of Volcano House; p. 109: Courtesy of Volcano House (top left, top right), © Stapleton Collection/Corbis (bottom); p. 111, 112: San Ysidro Ranch, A Rosewood Resort, © Rosewood Hotels & Resorts; p. 113: © Bettmann/Corbis (top left), San Ysidro Ranch, A Rosewood Resort, © Rosewood Hotels & Resorts (top right), © Kit Kittle/Corbis (bottom); p. 114–115: © Chuck Place/Alamy (left), © Bettmann/Corbis (center), San Ysidro Ranch, A Rosewood Resort, © Rosewood Hotels & Resorts (right), © Wildscape/Alamy (bottom); p. 117: Photo by Galen Rowell, courtesy of Post Ranch Inn; p. 118–119: photo by Kodiak Greenwood, courtesy of Post Ranch Inn (top left, top center, bottom right), © Tim Street-Porter/Beateworks/Corbis (top right), © John Cohen/Getty Images (bottom left); p. 120–121: © Allen Ginsberg/Corbis (top left), photo by Kodiak Greenwood, courtesy of Post Ranch Inn (top right), courtesy of Penguin Books (bottom); p. 123: Photo by Geraint Smith, courtesy of Mabel Dodge Luhan House; p. 124: Photo by Geraint Smith, courtesy of Mabel Dodge Luhan House (top), © Mary Evans Picture Library/Alamy (bottom right), © Bettmann/Corbis (bottom left); p. 125: © Mary Evans Picture Library/Alamy; p. 126: © Craig Aurness/Corbis; p. 127: © Paul Edmondson/Corbis (top), © Random House (bottom); p. 129: © Tim Street-Porter/Beateworks/Corbis; p. 130: Photo by Tim Street-Porter, courtesy of Chateau Marmont; p. 131: Michael Ochs Archives/Getty Images; p. 132: © Tim Street-Porter/Beateworks/Corbis (top, bottom right), photo by Nikolas Koenig, courtesy of Chateau Marmont (bottom left); p. 133: photo by Nikolas Koenig, courtesy of Chateau Marmont (top), *Rolling Stone* (bottom); p. 135: © Jeri Hines Photography; p. 136–137: © Robert Holmes/Corbis (left), *Evening Standard*/Getty Images (center), © Corbis (right); p. 138: © Jeri Hines Photography (top left), © Peter Horree/Alamy (top right), photo by Alfred Eisenstaedt, © Time & Life Pictures/Getty Images (bottom); p. 139: © Jeri Hines Photography (top), Courtesy of Maison de Ville (bottom); p. 141: Courtesy of Fairmont Hotels & Resorts; p. 142–143: © Rue des Archives/The Granger Collection, New York (left), courtesy of Fairmont Hotels & Resorts (center), courtesy of the Everett Collection (right); p. 144: Courtesy of Fairmont Hotels & Resorts; p. 145: Courtesy of the Everett Collection (left, bottom), courtesy of Fairmont Hotels & Resorts (right); p. 147: © Tim Street-Porter/Beateworks/Corbis; p. 149: © Geoffrey Weill Associates; p. 151: © Morgans Hotel Group; p. 153: © Solage Calistoga; p. 155: © The Standard Hotel, Los Angeles; p. 156–157: Courtesy of Ivy Hotel, p. 159: © The Standard Hotel, Los Angeles.

The Standard in Los Angeles.

ACKNOWLEDGMENTS

The publisher wishes to thank the following individuals for their contributions to this book: Courtney Abercrombie at the Maison de Ville; Ann Marie Basanese at Wenner Media; Jamie Beck at The Carlyle; Allison Benson at Morgans Hotel Group; Shannon Besoyan at Sun Valley Lodge; Becky Blaine at the Arizona Biltmore; Sabrina Bozek of Fairmont Hotels & Resorts; Lisa Burns at Saunders Hotel Group for The Lenox Hotel; Luc Alexis Chasleries; Yen Cheong at Viking and Penguin Books; Jordan Cole at Ivy Hotel; Clint and Julia Dickens at the Inn on Covered Bridge Green; Mathilde Dupuy D'Angeac; Sarah Hanson; Kristin Henn; Turi Hetherington at Rainbow Ranch Lodge; Miriam Hiersteiner; Jeri Hines of Jeri Hines Photography; Chian Hsu at Volcanoes Resort/Volcano House; Erika Imberti; Dilcia Johnson at Corbis; Roger Jones of Poolhouse Design; Stewart Lang and Anita Cotter for Amangani; April Louzek; Malick Kane at Getty Images; Esther Kremer; Ed Mari; Cyrene Mary; Keriann Greaney Martin, Lauren Ash Donoho, and Christine Donovan at Hotel del Coronado; Brian McCarthy at the Library of America; Meghan McGinnis and Jennifer Taverner at Nadine Johnson and Associates, Inc.; Jamie Myette at The Zimmerman Agency for Don CeSar Beach Resort; Lyndsey Ng at Penguin Press UK; Yann Popper; Silka Quintero of Granger Collection; Bonnie Reuben at The Breakers Palm Beach; Lucy Ridolphi at The Sundance Resort; Alison Jo Rigney at Everett Collection; John Rockwell; Jeanne L. Ross at Colorado Trails Ranch; Sajin Salim and Pradeep Kumar of Alamy; Perrine Scherrer; Geraint Smith; Shirley Springman at Curtis Publishing; Claire Tabek at The Biltmore; Teresa Tavares at Rosewood Hotels & Resorts for San Ysidro Ranch; Lucy Tran at Mission Ranch Carmel; Alicia M. Torello at Random House, Inc.; Bea Wolfe at Post Ranch Inn; Meredith Wright at Murphy O'Brien PR for the Solage; Karen Young at the Mabel Dodge Luhan House.

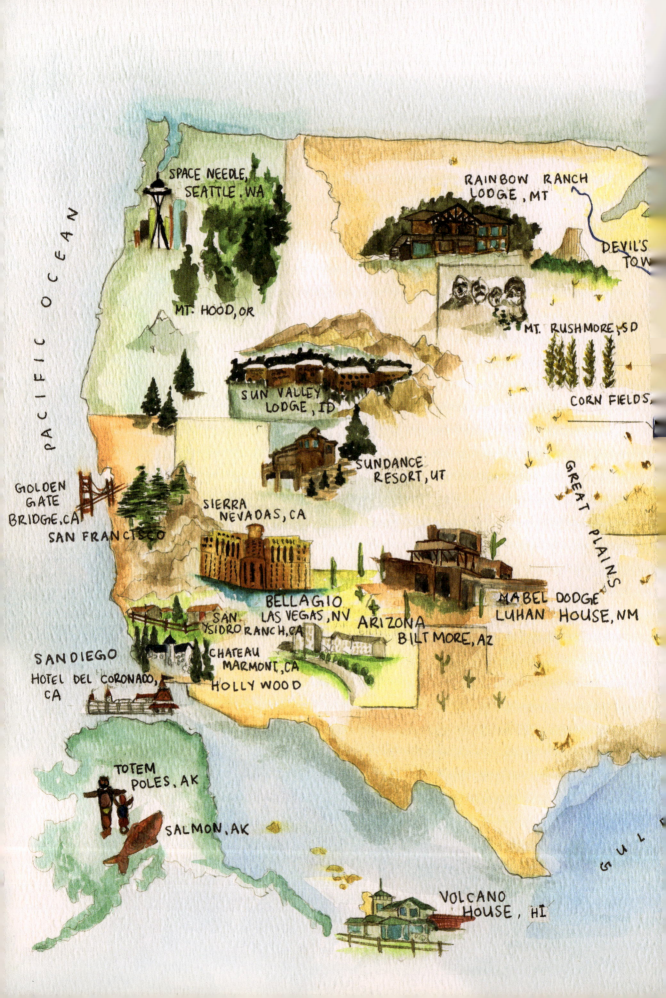

PACIFIC OCEAN

SPACE NEEDLE, SEATTLE, WA

MT. HOOD, OR

RAINBOW RANCH LODGE, MT

DEVIL'S TOW

MT. RUSHMORE, SD

CORN FIELDS,

SUN VALLEY LODGE, ID

SUNDANCE RESORT, UT

GREAT PLAINS

GOLDEN GATE BRIDGE, CA

SAN FRANCISCO

SIERRA NEVADAS, CA

BELLAGIO LAS VEGAS, NV

ARIZONA

MABEL DODGE LUHAN HOUSE, NM

SAN YSIDRO RANCH, CA

BILTMORE, AZ

SAN DIEGO

HOTEL DEL CORONADO, CA

CHATEAU MARMONT, CA

HOLLYWOOD

TOTEM POLES, AK

SALMON, AK

VOLCANO HOUSE, HI

GUL